Table of Contents

2

Place Value

Place value is the value of a digit, or numeral, shown by where it is in the number. For example, in 1,234, 1 has the place value of thousands, 2 is hundreds, 3 is tens, and 4 is ones.

Directions: Write the numbers in the correct boxes to find how far the car has traveled.

one thousand

six hundreds

eight ones

nine ten thousands

four tens

two millions

five hundred thousands

millions	hundred thousands	ten thousands	thousands	hundreds	tens	ones

How many miles has the car traveled? _____

Directions: In the number . . .

2,386 _____ is in the ones place.

4,957 _____ is in the hundreds place.

102,432 _____ is in the ten thousands place.

489,753 _____ is in the thousands place.

1,743,998 _____ is in the millions place.

Place Value: Standard Form

For this activity, you will need a number spinner or number cube.

Directions: Roll the cube or spin the spinner the same number of times as there are spaces in each place value box. The first number rolled or spun goes in the ones place, the second number in the tens place, and so on.

Example:

thousands	hundreds	tens	ones
4	5	6	7

Standard Form
4,567

hundreds	tens	ones

_____

thousands	hundreds	tens	ones

_____

ten thousands	thousands	hundreds	tens	ones

_____

hundred thousands	ten thousands	thousands	hundreds	tens	ones

_____

millions	hundred thousands	ten thousands	thousands	hundreds	tens	ones

_____

Directions: Write the number words for the numerals above.

_____

_____

_____

_____

Directions: Use the number cube or spinner to create numbers for the place value boxes below. Then, write the number in expanded notation and standard form.

Example:

thousands	hundreds	tens	ones
8	6	2	4

Standard Form __8,624__

Expanded Notation __8,000 + 600 + 20 + 4__

ten thousands	thousands	hundreds	tens	ones

Standard Form _____

Expanded Notation _____

ten thousands	thousands	hundreds	tens	ones

Standard Form _____

Expanded Notation _____

hundred thousands	ten thousands	thousands	hundreds	tens	ones

Standard Form _____

Expanded Notation _____

Directions: Write the value of the 4 in each number below.

742,521 _____

456 _____

65,504 _____

Add 'Em Up!

Addition is "putting together" or adding two or more numbers to find the sum.

Directions: Add the following problems as quickly as you can.

$$
\begin{array}{r} 3 \\ +2 \\ \hline \end{array}
\qquad
\begin{array}{r} 6 \\ +4 \\ \hline \end{array}
\qquad
\begin{array}{r} 5 \\ +4 \\ \hline \end{array}
\qquad
\begin{array}{r} 2 \\ +9 \\ \hline \end{array}
$$

$$
\begin{array}{r} 6 \\ +2 \\ \hline \end{array}
\qquad
\begin{array}{r} 4 \\ +1 \\ \hline \end{array}
\qquad
\begin{array}{r} 9 \\ +6 \\ \hline \end{array}
\qquad
\begin{array}{r} 7 \\ +6 \\ \hline \end{array}
\qquad
\begin{array}{r} 8 \\ +7 \\ \hline \end{array}
\qquad
\begin{array}{r} 8 \\ +9 \\ \hline \end{array}
$$

$$
\begin{array}{r} 9 \\ +4 \\ \hline \end{array}
\qquad
\begin{array}{r} 1 \\ +8 \\ \hline \end{array}
\qquad
\begin{array}{r} 4 \\ +7 \\ \hline \end{array}
\qquad
\begin{array}{r} 7 \\ +9 \\ \hline \end{array}
\qquad
\begin{array}{r} 5 \\ +6 \\ \hline \end{array}
\qquad
\begin{array}{r} 5 \\ +3 \\ \hline \end{array}
$$

$$
\begin{array}{r} 6 \\ +6 \\ \hline \end{array}
\qquad
\begin{array}{r} 8 \\ +8 \\ \hline \end{array}
\qquad
\begin{array}{r} 7 \\ +7 \\ \hline \end{array}
\qquad
\begin{array}{r} 4 \\ +4 \\ \hline \end{array}
$$

$$
\begin{array}{r} 2 \\ +8 \\ \hline \end{array}
\qquad
\begin{array}{r} 5 \\ +2 \\ \hline \end{array}
\qquad
\begin{array}{r} 5 \\ +6 \\ \hline \end{array}
\qquad
\begin{array}{r} 5 \\ +8 \\ \hline \end{array}
$$

How quickly did you complete this page? _____

Directions: Play the following addition games to practice your math facts.

1. ROLL 'EM!

For one or more players.

Materials: two number cubes or dice or two number spinners per player

How to play: Each player rolls his or her number cubes (dice) or spins his or her spinners simultaneously. As quickly as possible, he or she adds the two numbers rolled or spun. Whoever is first to add the numbers correctly wins the round.

2. ADD 'EM!

For one or more players.

Materials: addition flash cards

How to play: An adult shows the flash cards one at a time to each player, who solves the addition problem. Place correctly answered cards in one stack and incorrectly answered cards in another. Which stack is larger? Try again. This time try to answer all the cards correctly.

Going in Circles

Directions: Where the circles meet, write the sum of the numbers from the circles on the right and left and above and below. The first one shows you what to do.

Leafy Addition

Directions: Add, then color according to the code.

Code:

green — 79   orange — 35   red — 78

yellow — 87   purple — 56   brown — 94

$$57 + 21$$

$$34 + 22$$

$$23 + 12$$

$$35 + 52$$

$$15 + 41$$

$$62 + 32$$

$$20 + 74$$

$$34 + 44$$

$$56 + 23$$

$$47 + 40$$

$$27 + 8$$

$$63 + 16$$

Magic Squares

Directions: Some of the number squares below are "magic" and some are not. Squares that add up to the same number horizontally, vertically, and diagonally are "magic." Add the numbers horizontally and vertically in each square to discover which ones are "magic."

Example:

1.
4	9	2	15
3	5	7	15
8	1	6	15
15	15	15	15

Magic? __yes__

1.
7	2	1
3	4	8
5	9	6

Magic? _____

2.
6	11	4
5	7	9
10	3	8

Magic? _____

3.
3	8	1
2	4	6
7	0	5

Magic? _____

4.
2	7	0
1	3	5
6	9	4

Magic? _____

5.
5	10	3
4	6	8
9	2	7

Magic? _____

6.
7	12	5
6	8	10
11	4	9

Magic? _____

7.
1	2	3
4	5	6
7	8	9

Magic? _____

8.
6	7	4
1	5	9
8	3	2

Magic? _____

Challenge: Can you discover a pattern for number placement in the magic squares? Try to make a magic square of your own.

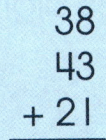

Directions: Add or subtract, using regrouping when needed.

38	1,269		629	
43	2,453	5,792	491	4,697
+ 21	+ 8,219	− 4,814	+ 308	− 2,988

	68	197		
5,280	27	436	7,321	456
− 3,147	+ 42	+ 213	− 2,789	+ 974

	492			
3,932	863	9,873	4,978	6,235
+ 4,681	+ 57	+ 5,483	+ 2,131	+ 2,986

Sue stocked her pond with 263 bass and 187 trout. The turtles ate 97 fish. How many fish are left?

_____

Rounding: Tens

Rounding a number means expressing it to the nearest ten, hundred, thousand, and so on. Rounding makes estimating sums, differences, and products easier. When rounding to the nearest ten, the key number is in the ones place. If the ones digit is 5 or larger, round up to the nearest ten. If the ones digit is 4 or less, round down to the nearest ten.

Example:
Round 81 to the nearest ten.
• 1 is the key digit.
• If it is less than 5, round down.
• Answer: 80

Directions:
Round these numbers to the nearest ten.

41 32 75 481 165 29 89 17 38 68 52 87 573 98 43 12

Rounding: Hundreds and Thousands

When rounding to the nearest hundred, the key number is in the tens place. If the tens digit is 5 or larger, round up to the nearest hundred. If the tens digit is 4 or less, round down to the nearest hundred.

Examples:

Round 871 to the nearest hundred.
- 7 is the key digit.
- If it is 5 or more, round up.
- Answer: 900

Round 421 to the nearest hundred.
- 2 is the key digit.
- If it is 4 or less, round down.
- Answer: 400

Directions: Round these numbers to the nearest hundred.

255 _____   368 _____

578 _____   562 _____

99 _____   775 _____

When rounding to the nearest thousand, the key number is in the hundreds place. If the hundreds digit is 5 or larger, round up to the nearest thousand. If the hundreds digit is 4 or less, round down to the nearest thousand.

Examples:

Round 7,932 to the nearest thousand.
- 9 is the key digit.
- If it is 5 or more, round up.
- Answer: 8,000

Round 1,368 to the nearest thousand.
- 3 is the key digit.
- If it is 4 or less, round down.
- Answer: 1,000

Directions: Round these numbers to the nearest thousand.

8,631 _____   1,248 _____   798 _____

999 _____   6,229 _____   8,461 _____

Rounding

Directions: Round these numbers to the nearest ten.

18 _____   33 _____   82 _____   56 _____

24 _____   49 _____   91 _____   67 _____

Directions: Round these numbers to the nearest hundred.

243 _____   689 _____   263 _____

162 _____   389 _____   720 _____

351 _____   490 _____   463 _____

846 _____   928 _____   733 _____

Directions: Round these numbers to the nearest thousand.

2,638 _____   3,940 _____   8,653 _____

6,238 _____   1,429 _____   5,061 _____

7,289 _____   2,742 _____   9,460 _____

3,109 _____   4,697 _____   8,302 _____

Directions: Round these numbers to the nearest ten thousand.

11,368 _____   38,421 _____

75,302 _____   67,932 _____

14,569 _____   49,926 _____

93,694 _____   81,648 _____

26,784 _____   87,065 _____

To **estimate** means to give an approximate rather than an exact answer. To find an estimated sum or difference, round the numbers of the problem, then add or subtract. If the number has 5 ones or more, round up to the nearest ten. If the number has 4 ones or less, round down to the nearest ten.

Directions: Round the numbers to the nearest ten, hundred, or thousand. Then, add or subtract.

Examples:

Ten	Hundred	Thousand
74 → 70 + 39 → + 40 ——— 110	352 → 400 – 164 → – 200 ——— 200	7,681 → 8,000 + 4,321 → + 4,000 ——— 12,000

Round these numbers to the nearest ten.

$$18 \rightarrow$$
$$+ 24 \rightarrow$$

$$49 \rightarrow$$
$$- 33 \rightarrow$$

$$67 \rightarrow$$
$$- 56 \rightarrow$$

Round these numbers to the nearest hundred.

$$255 \rightarrow$$
$$- 99 \rightarrow$$

$$526 \rightarrow$$
$$+ 145 \rightarrow$$

$$102 \rightarrow$$
$$- 75 \rightarrow$$

Round these numbers to the nearest thousand.

$$8,361 \rightarrow$$
$$+ 889 \rightarrow$$

$$9,926 \rightarrow$$
$$+ 3,645 \rightarrow$$

Estimating

Estimating is used for certain mathematical calculations. For example, to figure the cost of several items, round their prices to the nearest dollar, then add up the approximate cost. A store clerk, on the other hand, needs to know the exact prices in order to charge the correct amount.

Directions: In the following situations, write whether an exact or estimated answer should be used.

Example:

You make a deposit in your bank account. Do you want an estimated total or an exact total?

Exact

1. Your family just ate dinner at a restaurant. Your parents are trying to calculate the tip for your server. Should they estimate by rounding or use exact numbers?

   _____

2. You are at the store buying a book, and you want to know if you have enough money to pay for it. Should you estimate or use exact numbers?

   _____

3. Some friends are planning a trip from New York City to Washington, D.C. They need to know about how far they will travel in miles. Should they estimate or use exact numbers?

   _____

4. You plan a trip to the zoo. Beforehand, you call the zoo for the price of admission. Should the person at the zoo tell you an estimated or exact price?

   _____

Estimating

Directions: Round the numbers to the nearest hundred. Then, solve the problems.

Example:

Jack and Alex were playing a computer game. Jack scored 428 points. Alex scored 132. About how many more points did Jack score than Alex?

Round Jack's 428 points down to the nearest hundred, 400.

Round Alex's 132 points down to 100.

Subtract.

$$\begin{array}{r} 400 \\ -\ 100 \\ \hline \textbf{estimate}\quad 300 \end{array}$$

258 → 300 + 117 → + 100 375 400	493 → + 114 →	837 → − 252 →
928 → − 437 →	700 → − 491 →	319 → + 630 →
332 → + 567 →	493 → − 162 →	1,356 → + 2,941 →

Estimating

Directions: Follow the steps to estimate the time it will take to read a book.

Step 1: Write down the number of pages in the book you want to read.

_____

Step 2: Pick a page that is of average length. Time yourself to see how long it takes you to read the page.

_____

Step 3: Suppose it took you 4 minutes to read the page. How many minutes will it take to read the book?

_____

Step 4: Estimate the number of minutes it will take to read the book by rounding up to the nearest hundred.

_____

Skip counting is a quick way to count by skipping numbers. For example, when you skip count by twos, you count 2, 4, 6, 8, and so on. You can skip count by many different numbers such as twos, fours, fives, tens, and hundreds.

The illustration below shows skip counting to 14.

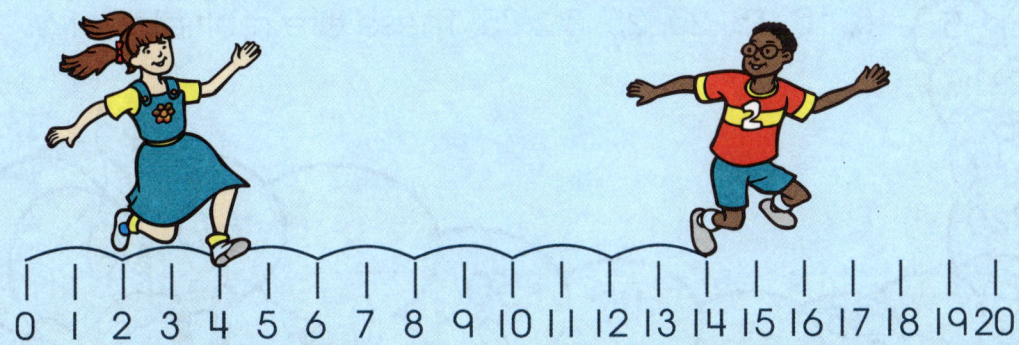

0 1 2 3 4 5 6 7 8 9 10 11 12 13 14 15 16 17 18 19 20

Directions: Use the number line to help you skip count by twos from 0 to 20.

0, ____, ____, ____, 8, ____, ____, 14, ____, ____, ____

Directions: Skip count by threes by filling in the rocks across the pond.

Multiples

A multiple is the product of a specific number and any other number. For example, the multiples of 2 are 2 (2 x 1), 4 (2 x 2), 6, 8, 10, 12, and so on.

Directions: Write the missing multiples.

Example: Count by fives.
5, 10, 15, 20, 25, 30, 35. These are multiples of 5.

Review

Directions: Add or subtract using regrouping.

```
  67
  93            5,029          732           2,467         8,453
+ 48          - 3,068        + 18          + 3,184       - 6,087
```

Directions: Write the numbers in the boxes. In the blanks, write the numbers in standard form.

eight millions, four hundred thousands, zero ten thousands, zero thousands, nine hundreds, five tens, two ones

millions	hundred thousands	ten thousands	thousands	hundreds	tens	ones

_____

five hundred thousands, three ten thousands, five thousands, zero hundreds, four tens, one one

hundred thousands	ten thousands	thousands	hundreds	tens	ones

_____

Directions: Write the missing multiples in the blanks.

6, 12, 18, _____, 30, _____   3, _____, _____, 12, 15

4, _____, 12, 16, _____, 24   _____, 10, 15, _____, _____

Multiplication

Multiplication is a short way to find the sum of adding the same number a certain amount of times, such as 7 x 4 = 28 instead of 7 + 7 + 7 + 7 = 28.

Directions: Multiply as quickly as you can.

4	7	0	7	9	1
x 7	x 6	x 8	x 2	x 5	x 5

8	7	4	9	8	6
x 3	x 1	x 2	x 6	x 5	x 7

3	7	3	5	9	7
x 5	x 8	x 9	x 6	x 9	x 5

3	2	8
x 6	x 8	x 6

0	3
x 7	x 3

How quickly did you complete this page? _____

Fact Factory

Factors are the numbers multiplied together in a multiplication problem. The **product** is the answer.

Directions: Write the missing factors or products.

x	5
1	5
5	
4	20
6	
3	
2	10
7	
9	45

x	9
8	72
3	
4	
9	
6	54
7	
2	
1	9

x	7
2	14
5	
	42
8	
7	
4	
	21
0	

x	3
7	
4	
6	
1	
3	
2	
5	
8	

x	1
1	
12	
10	
3	3
5	
7	
6	
4	

x	8
9	
8	
4	
5	
6	
7	
3	
2	

x	2
	24
2	
22	
4	
20	
6	
18	
8	

x	4
2	
4	
6	
8	
	4
	12
	20
	28

x	6
7	
6	
5	
4	
3	
2	
1	
0	

x	10
	20
3	
	40
5	
	60
7	
	80
9	

x	11
4	
7	
9	
10	
3	
5	
6	
8	

x	12
1	
2	24
3	
4	48
5	
6	
7	
8	

Multiplication: Tens, Hundreds, Thousands

When multiplying a number by 10, the answer is the number with a 0. It is like counting by tens.

Examples:

$$\begin{array}{r} 10 \\ \times\ 1 \\ \hline 10 \end{array} \qquad \begin{array}{r} 10 \\ \times\ 2 \\ \hline 20 \end{array} \qquad \begin{array}{r} 10 \\ \times\ 3 \\ \hline 30 \end{array} \qquad \begin{array}{r} 10 \\ \times\ 4 \\ \hline 40 \end{array} \qquad \begin{array}{r} 10 \\ \times\ 5 \\ \hline 50 \end{array} \qquad \begin{array}{r} 10 \\ \times\ 6 \\ \hline 60 \end{array}$$

When multiplying a number by 100, the answer is the number with two 0's. When multiplying by 1,000, the answer is the number with three 0's.

Examples:

$$\begin{array}{r} 100 \\ \times\ 1 \\ \hline 100 \end{array} \qquad \begin{array}{r} 100 \\ \times\ 2 \\ \hline 200 \end{array} \qquad \begin{array}{r} 100 \\ \times\ 3 \\ \hline 300 \end{array} \qquad \begin{array}{r} 1,000 \\ \times\ 1 \\ \hline 1,000 \end{array} \qquad \begin{array}{r} 1,000 \\ \times\ 2 \\ \hline 2,000 \end{array} \qquad \begin{array}{r} 1,000 \\ \times\ 3 \\ \hline 3,000 \end{array}$$

Directions: Multiply.

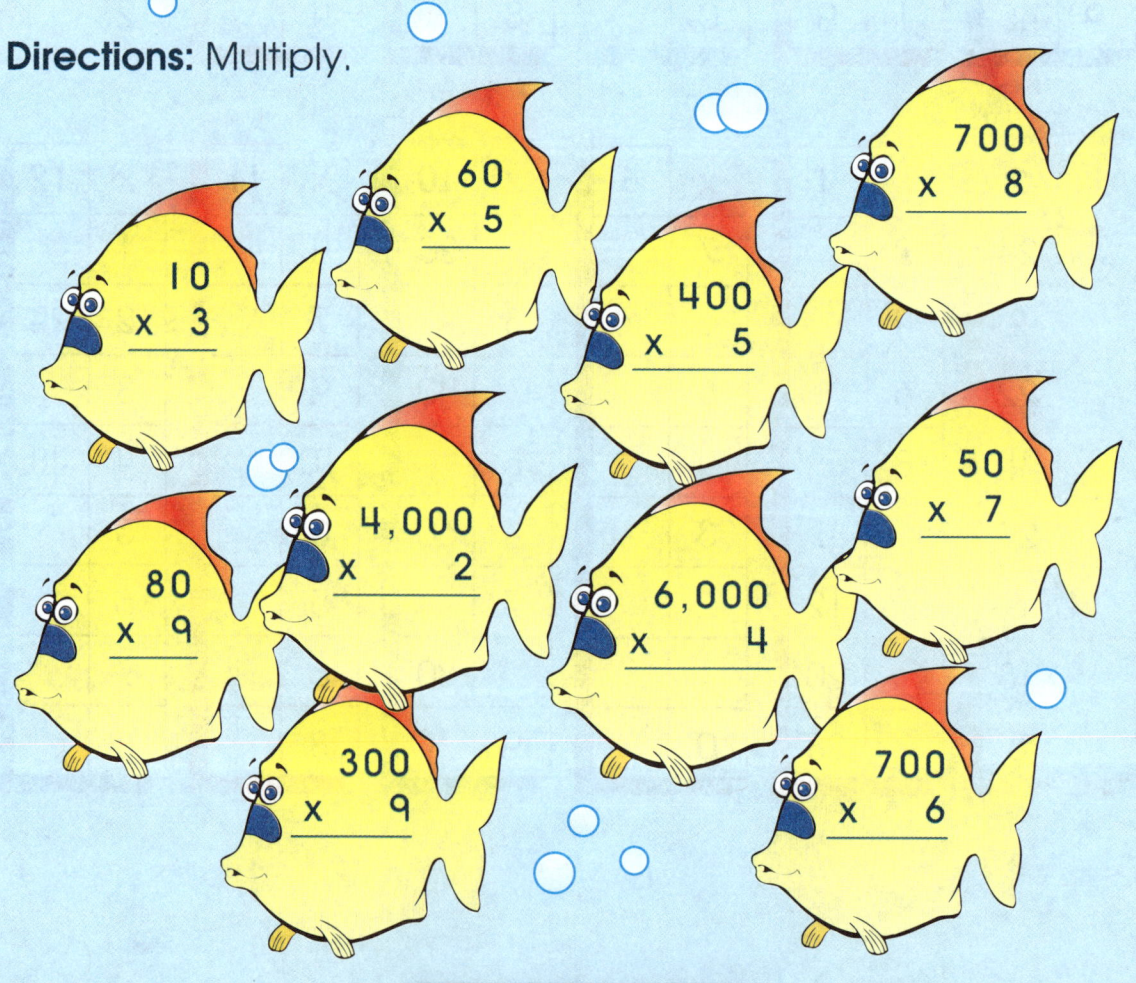

$$\begin{array}{r} 10 \\ \times\ 3 \\ \hline \end{array} \qquad \begin{array}{r} 60 \\ \times\ 5 \\ \hline \end{array} \qquad \begin{array}{r} 400 \\ \times\ 5 \\ \hline \end{array} \qquad \begin{array}{r} 700 \\ \times\ 8 \\ \hline \end{array}$$

$$\begin{array}{r} 80 \\ \times\ 9 \\ \hline \end{array} \qquad \begin{array}{r} 4,000 \\ \times\ 2 \\ \hline \end{array} \qquad \begin{array}{r} 6,000 \\ \times\ 4 \\ \hline \end{array} \qquad \begin{array}{r} 50 \\ \times\ 7 \\ \hline \end{array}$$

$$\begin{array}{r} 300 \\ \times\ 9 \\ \hline \end{array} \qquad \begin{array}{r} 700 \\ \times\ 6 \\ \hline \end{array}$$

Follow the steps for multiplying a one-digit number by a two-digit number using regrouping.

Example: **Step 1:**   Multiply the ones. Regroup.

$$\begin{array}{r} \overset{2}{5}4 \\ \times\ 7 \\ \hline 8 \end{array}$$

Step 2:   Multiply the tens. Add two tens.

$$\begin{array}{r} \overset{2}{5}4 \\ \times\ 7 \\ \hline 378 \end{array}$$

Directions: Multiply.

27 x 3	63 x 4	52 x 5	91 x 9	45 x 7
64 x 5	76 x 3	93 x 6	87 x 4	66 x 7
		47 x 8	64 x 9	51 x 8
		13 x 7	32 x 4	25 x 8

The chickens on the Smith farm produce 48 dozen eggs each day. How many dozen eggs do they produce in 7 days? _____

Follow the steps for multiplying a two-digit number by a two-digit number using regrouping.

Example: **Step 1:**   Multiply the ones. Regroup.

$$
\begin{array}{r} 63 \\ \times\ 68 \\ \hline \end{array}
\qquad
\begin{array}{r} \overset{2}{6}3 \\ \times\ 68 \\ \hline 504 \end{array}
$$

Step 2:   Multiply the tens. Regroup. Add.

$$
\begin{array}{r} \overset{1}{6}3 \\ \times\ 68 \\ \hline 3{,}780 \end{array}
\qquad
\begin{array}{r} 63 \\ \times\ 68 \\ \hline 504 \\ +\ 3{,}780 \\ \hline 4{,}284 \end{array}
$$

Hint: When multiplying by the tens, start writing the number in the tens place. Use a zero as a placeholder in the ones place.

Directions: Multiply.

12 x 55	27 x 15	65 x 27	19 x 39	99 x 13
43 x 26	38 x 17	53 x 86	47 x 72	57 x 62

The Jones farm has 24 cows that each produce 52 quarts of milk a day. How many quarts are produced each day altogether?

_____

Follow the steps for multiplying a two-digit number by a three-digit number using regrouping.

Example:

Step 1: Multiply the ones. Regroup.

```
        287        2 2
      x  43        287
                 x  43
                   861
```

Step 2: Multiply the tens. Regroup. Add.

```
        3 2
        287        287
      x  43      x  43
     11,480        861
                + 11,480
                  12,341
```

Directions: Multiply.

```
  434          357
x  48        x  75
```

```
  231          754          614
x  46        x  65        x  59
```

```
  372          458
x  94        x  85
```

At the Douglas berry farm, workers pick 378 baskets of peaches each day. Each basket holds 65 peaches. How many peaches are picked each day? _____

Multiplication: Two-Digit Numbers Times Two- and Three-Digit Numbers

Directions: Multiply.

25 x 72	70 x 66	844 x 24	124 x 15
	45 x 41	76 x 78	74 x 69
	261 x 88	48 x 36	263 x 57
	37 x 64	52 x 43	321 x 78
	544 x 58	797 x 24	998 x 37

Multiplication: Two-Digit Numbers Times Three-Digit Numbers

Directions: Multiply. Regroup when needed.

Example:

```
     563
  x  248
  -------
   4,504
  22,520
+112,600
  -------
 139,624
```

Hint: When multiplying by the tens, start writing the number in the tens place. When multiplying by the hundreds, start in the hundreds place.

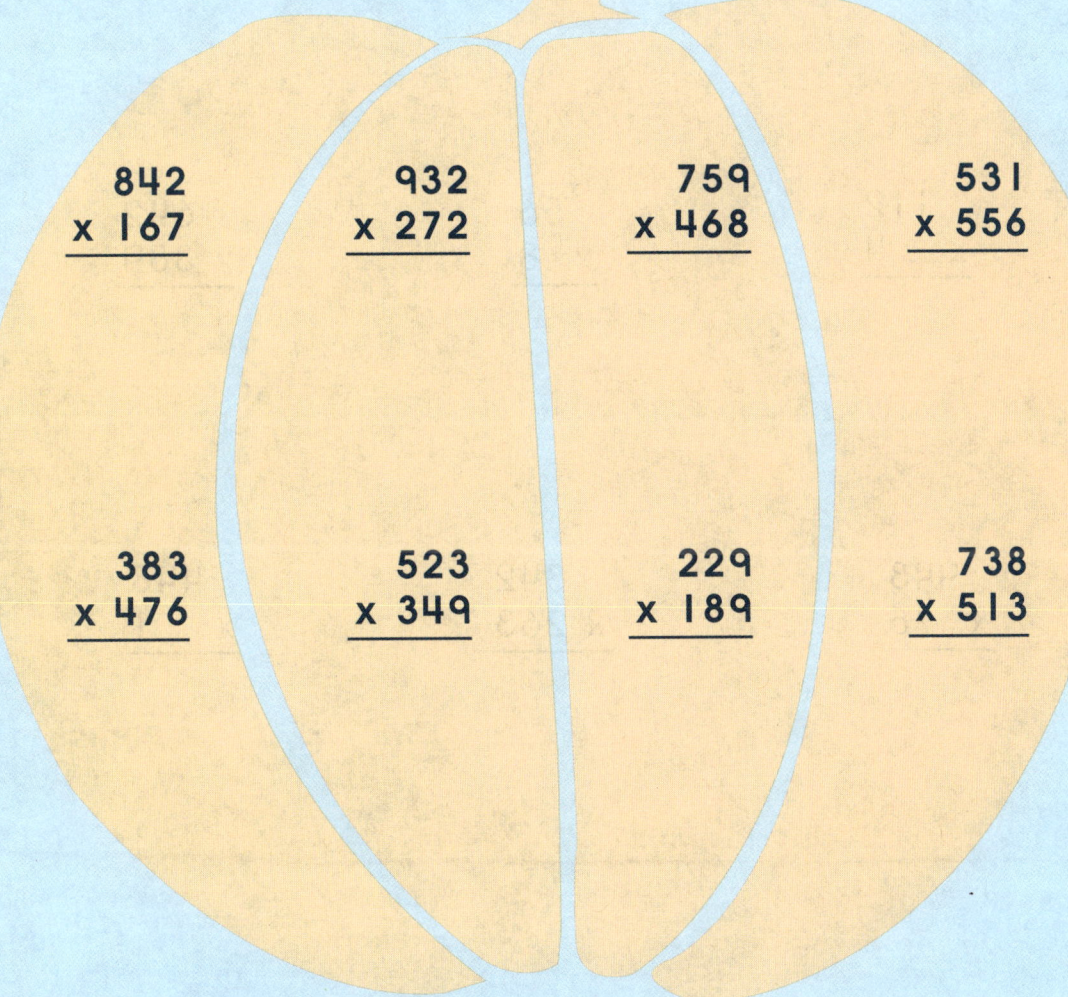

```
  842        932        759        531
x 167      x 272      x 468      x 556
```

```
  383        523        229        738
x 476      x 349      x 189      x 513
```

James grows pumpkins on his farm. He has 362 rows of pumpkins. There are 593 pumpkins in each row. How many pumpkins does James grow? _____

Multiplication Practice

Directions: Multiply. Use the code to color the quilt.

70,725 — **red**	667 — **green**	448 — **white**
249,738 — **orange**	34,088 — **blue**	221,446 — **yellow**

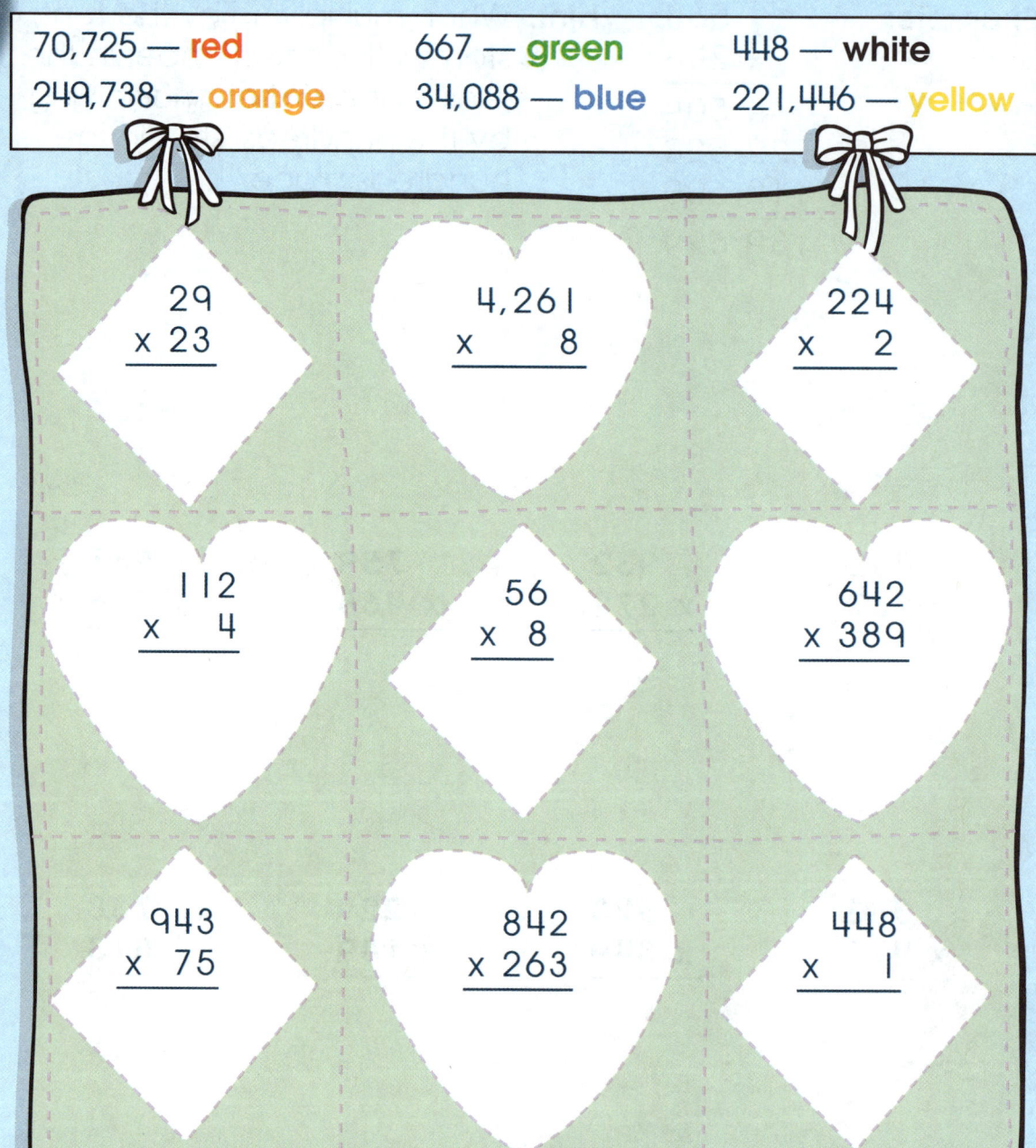

$$\begin{array}{r} 29 \\ \times\ 23 \\ \hline \end{array}$$

$$\begin{array}{r} 4,261 \\ \times\ \ \ \ \ 8 \\ \hline \end{array}$$

$$\begin{array}{r} 224 \\ \times\ \ \ \ 2 \\ \hline \end{array}$$

$$\begin{array}{r} 112 \\ \times\ \ \ \ 4 \\ \hline \end{array}$$

$$\begin{array}{r} 56 \\ \times\ \ 8 \\ \hline \end{array}$$

$$\begin{array}{r} 642 \\ \times\ 389 \\ \hline \end{array}$$

$$\begin{array}{r} 943 \\ \times\ \ 75 \\ \hline \end{array}$$

$$\begin{array}{r} 842 \\ \times\ 263 \\ \hline \end{array}$$

$$\begin{array}{r} 448 \\ \times\ \ \ \ 1 \\ \hline \end{array}$$

Directions: Multiply.

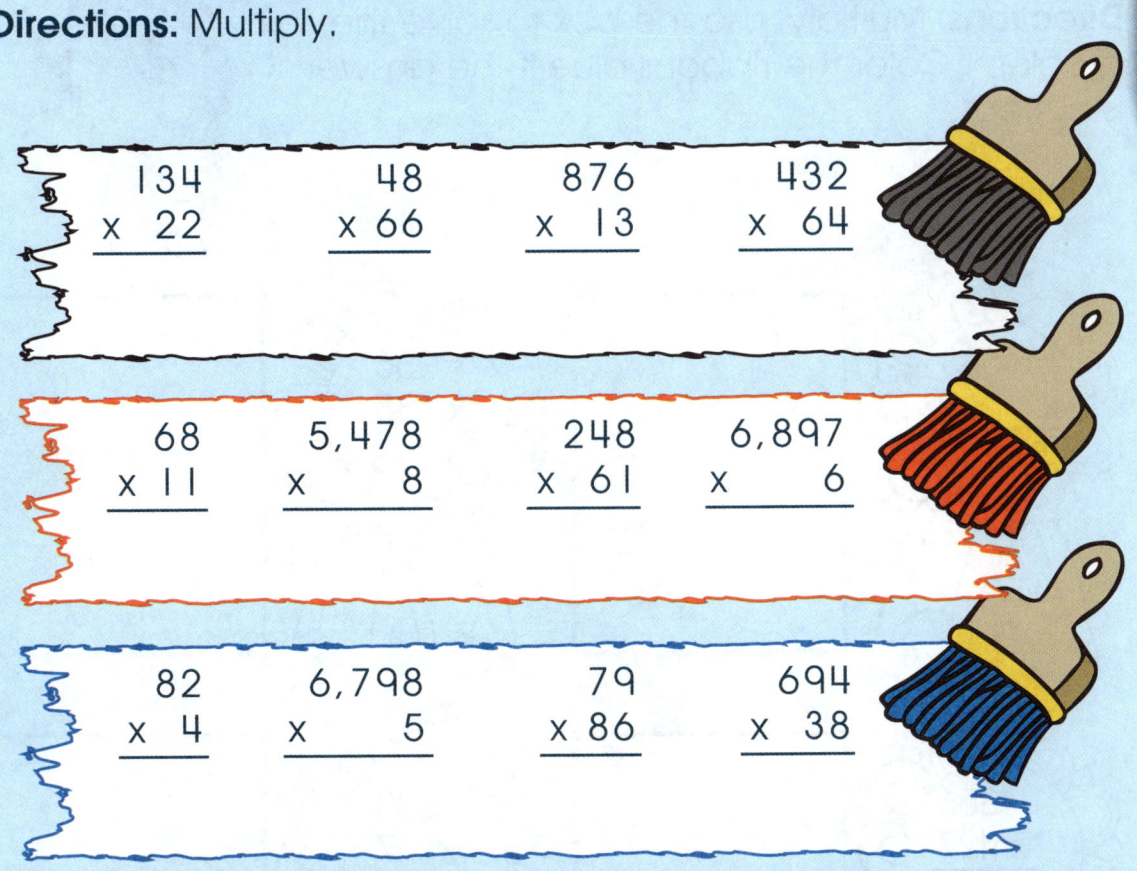

134 x 22	48 x 66	876 x 13	432 x 64
68 x 11	5,478 x 8	248 x 61	6,897 x 6
82 x 4	6,798 x 5	79 x 86	694 x 38

Directions: Color the picture by matching each number with its paintbrush.

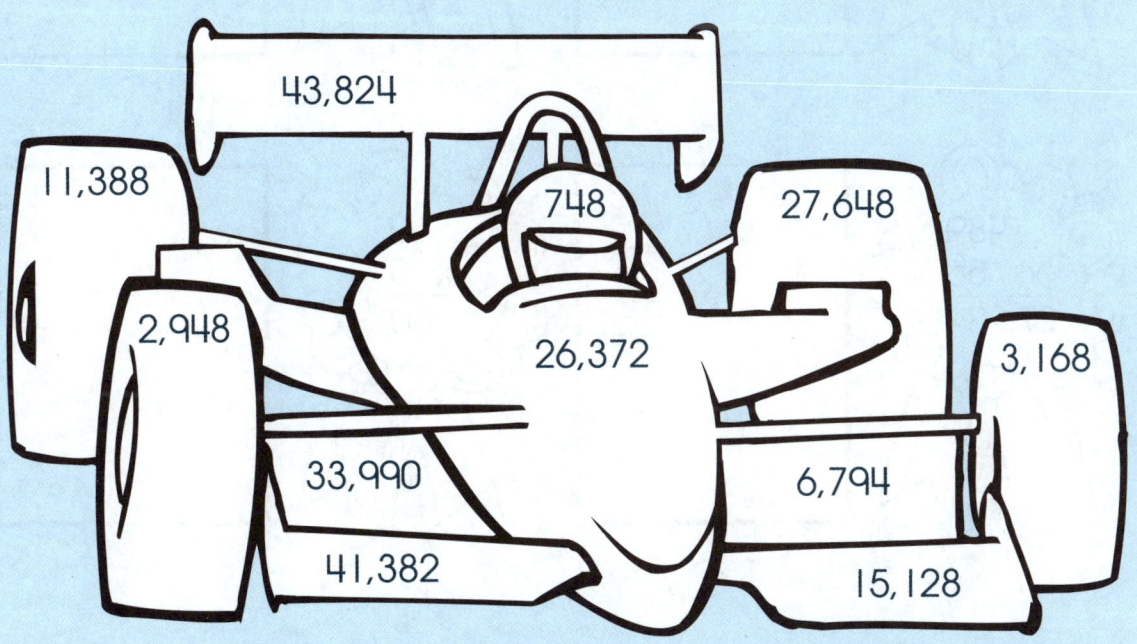

43,824

11,388

748

27,648

2,948

26,372

3,168

33,990

6,794

41,382

15,128

Review

Directions: Multiply. Use the box to solve the problem. Color the ribbons blue if the answer is correct.

5,683
x   9
51,147

256
x   38
8,728

356
x 427
152,012

800
x   7
6,300

489
x   56
27,284

60
x 5
300

Division

Division is a way to find out how many times one number is contained in another number. For example, 28 ÷ 7 = 4 means that there are 4 groups of 7 in 28.

Division problems can be written two ways: 36 ÷ 6 or 6)̄36

These are the parts of a division problem:

dividend ⟶ 36 ÷ 6 = 6
                  ↑   ↖
              divisor quotient

6 ← quotient
6)̄36 ← dividend
↑
divisor

Directions: Divide.

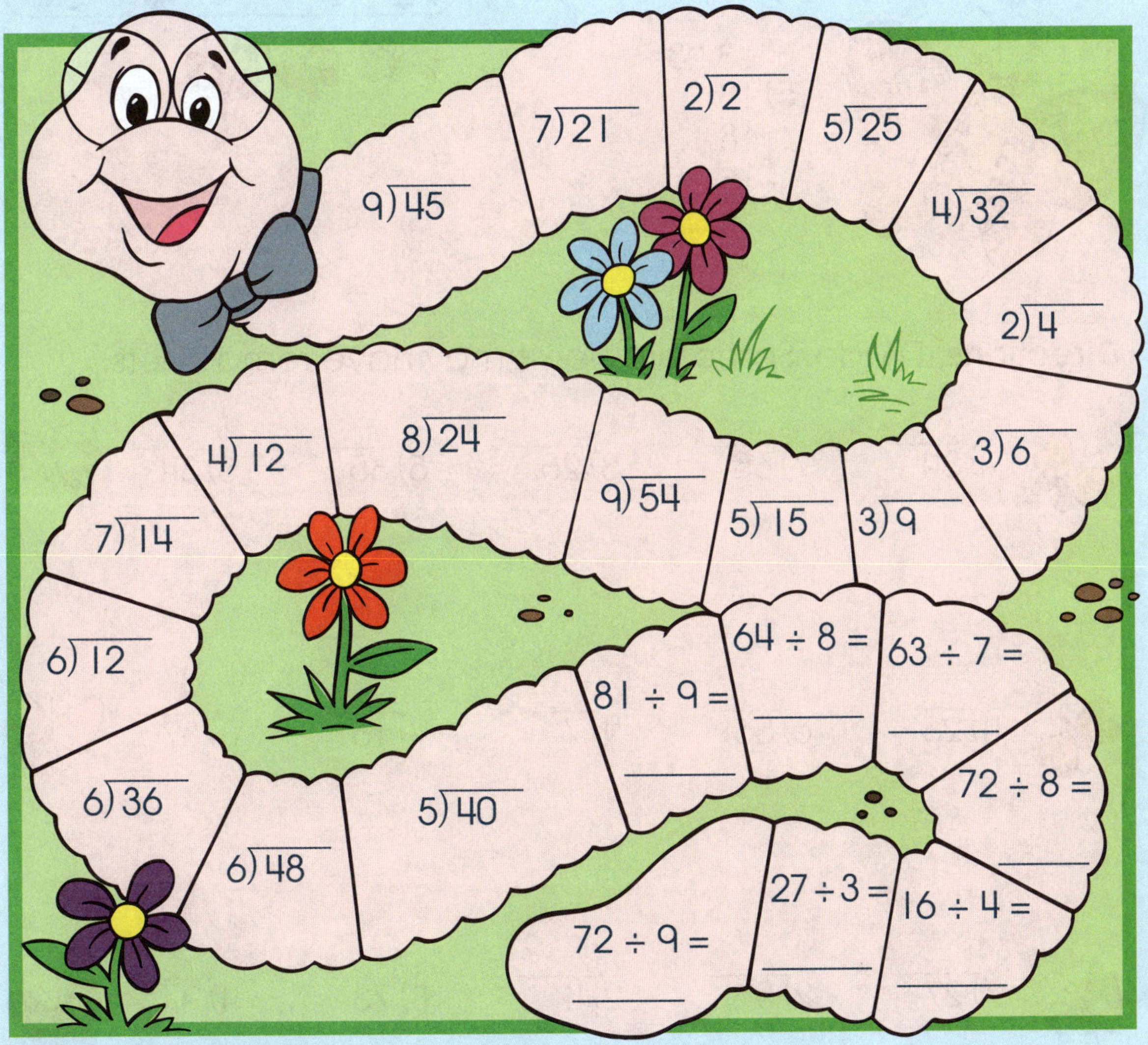

7)21   2)2   5)25

9)45   4)32

2)4

4)12   8)24   3)6

9)54   5)15   3)9

7)14

6)12

64 ÷ 8 =   63 ÷ 7 =

81 ÷ 9 = _____

72 ÷ 8 =

6)36   5)40

6)48

27 ÷ 3 =   16 ÷ 4 =

72 ÷ 9 =

Division With Remainders

Sometimes groups of objects or numbers cannot be divided into equal groups. The **remainder** is the number left over in the quotient of a division problem. The remainder must be smaller than the divisor.

Example:

Divide 18 butterflies into groups of 5. You have 3 equal groups, with 3 butterflies left over.

$$18 \div 5 = 3 \text{ R}3$$

or

$$\begin{array}{r} 3 \text{ R}3 \\ 5\overline{)18} \\ 18 \\ -15 \\ \hline 3 \end{array}$$

Directions: Divide. Some problems may have remainders.

 $9\overline{)84}$ $7\overline{)65}$ $8\overline{)25}$ $5\overline{)35}$ $5\overline{)34}$

 $4\overline{)25}$ $6\overline{)56}$ $4\overline{)7}$ $4\overline{)16}$ $8\overline{)37}$

 $7\overline{)27}$ $2\overline{)5}$ $2\overline{)4}$ $8\overline{)73}$ $4\overline{)9}$

Division: Larger Numbers

Follow the steps for dividing larger numbers.

Example: 3)66

Step 1: Divide the tens first.

```
    2
3)66
 - 6
   06
```

Step 2: Divide the ones next.

```
   22
3)66
 - 6
   06
  - 6
    0
```

Directions: Divide.

4)84   2)90   2)64   2)50   3)45

In some larger numbers, the divisor goes into the first two digits of the dividend.

Example:

```
9)729
```

```
    8
9)729
 -72
   09
```

```
   81
9)729
 -72
   09
  - 9
    0
```

Directions: Divide.

7)630   5)125   6)486   5)100   6)540

Division

Directions: Divide.

7)860   6)611   8)279   4)338

6)979   3)792   5)463   6)940

4)647   3)814   7)758   5)356

The music store has 491 CDs. The store sells 8 CDs a day. How many days will it take to sell all of the CDs?

_____

Division: Checking the Answers

To check a division problem, multiply the quotient by the divisor. Add the remainder. The answer will be the dividend.

Example:

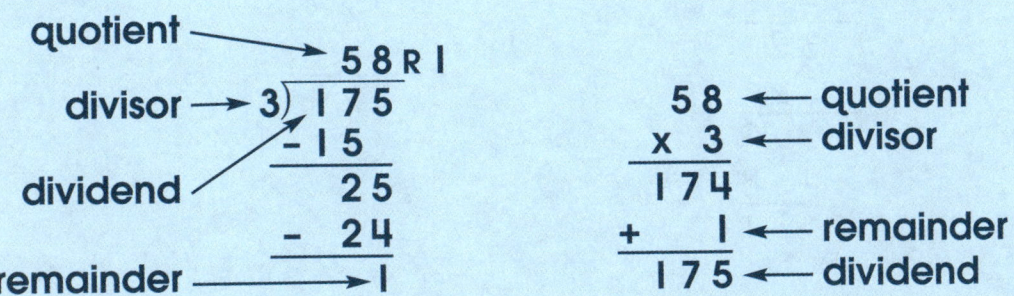

Directions: Divide each problem, then draw a line from the division problem to the correct checking problem.

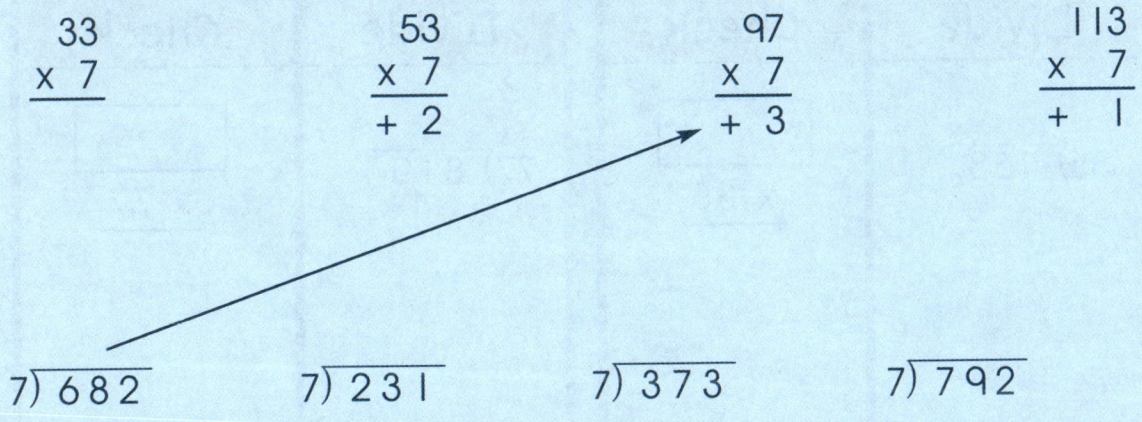

33	53	97	113
x 7	x 7	x 7	x 7
	+ 2	+ 3	+ 1

7) 682   7) 231   7) 373   7) 792

The toy factory puts 7 robot dogs in each box. The factory has 256 robot dogs. How many boxes will they need?

_____

Division: Checking the Answers

Directions: Divide, then check your answers.

Example:
```
     1 8 2 R 1
  4) 7 2 9
   - 4
     3 2
   - 3 2
        9
      - 8
        1
```

Check:
```
     1 8 2
   x     4
     7 2 8
   +     1
     7 2 9
```

Divide	Check	Divide	Check
35) 468	 ▢ x 35	77) 819	▢ x 77
29) 568	▢ x 29	53) 2,795	▢ x 53

The bookstore puts 53 books on a shelf. How many shelves will it need for 1,590 books? _____

Division: One-Digit Divisors

Directions: Solve the problems on another sheet of paper. Use the code to color the picture.

Color	$5\overline{)895}$	$6\overline{)895}$	$6\overline{)940}$	$4\overline{)647}$	orange
these	$4\overline{)672}$	$6\overline{)696}$	$5\overline{)749}$	$8\overline{)628}$	blue
answers:	$3\overline{)814}$	$7\overline{)490}$	$5\overline{)398}$	$2\overline{)571}$	black

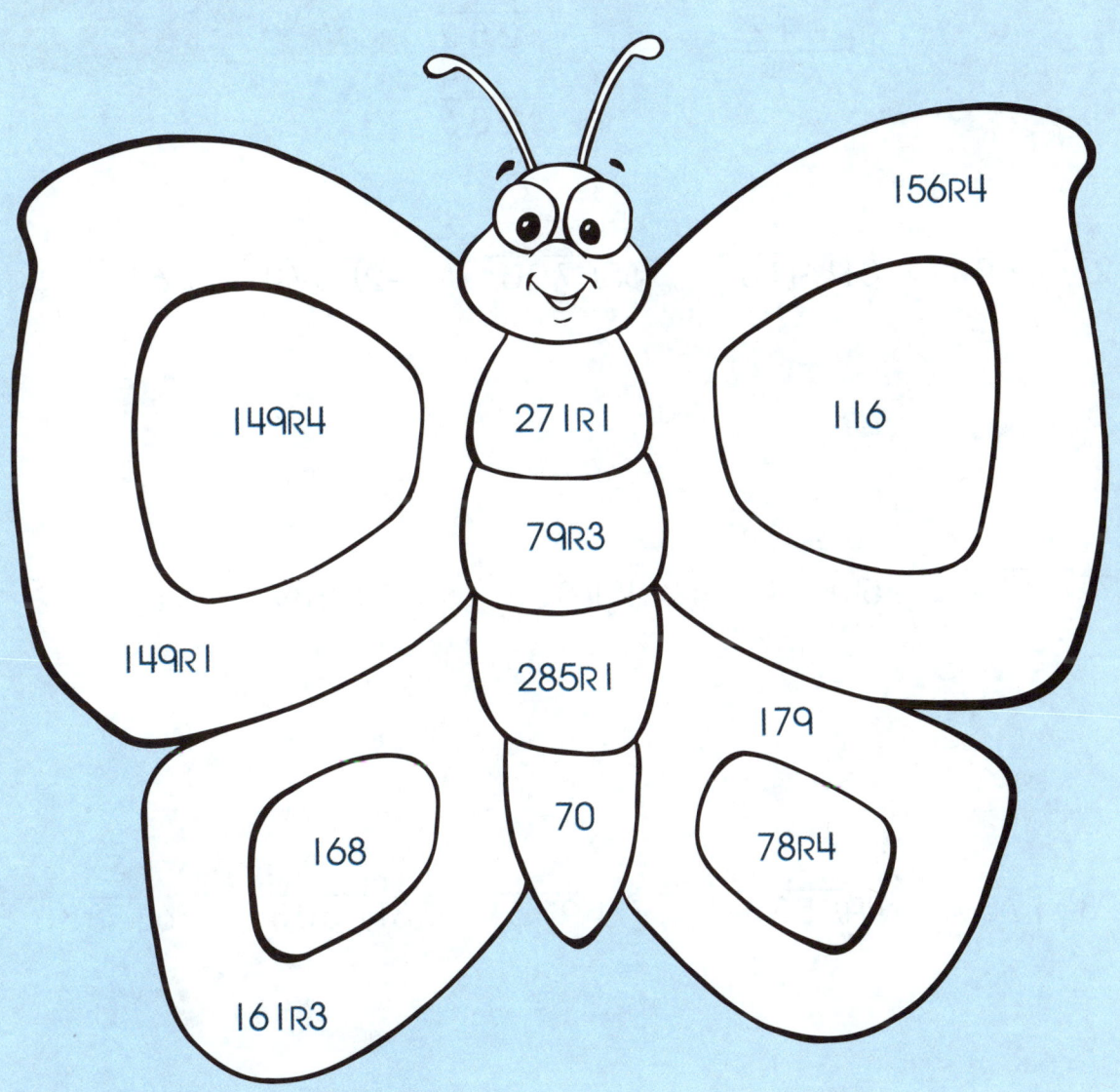

156R4

149R4

271R1

116

79R3

149R1

285R1

179

70

168

78R4

161R3

Directions: Divide. Then, check each answer on another sheet of paper by multiplying it by the divisor and adding the remainder.

Example:

```
         2                  21 R4
    12) 256             12) 256
      - 24                 - 24
        1                    16
                           - 12
                             4
```

Check:

```
     21
   x 12
     42
   2 1 0
   2 5 2
 +     4
   2 5 6
```

27) 880   81) 913   65) 790   42) 674   67) 823

72) 977   54) 743   45) 863   24) 432   18) 372

28) 175   49) 538   77) 936   37) 603   63) 835

The Allen farm has 882 chickens. The chickens are kept in 21 coops. How many chickens are there in each coop? _____

Averaging

An **average** is found by adding two or more quantities and dividing by the number of quantities.

Example:

Step 1: Find the sum of the numbers. 24 + 36 + 30 = 90

Step 2: Divide by the number of quantities. 90 ÷ 3 = 30

The average is 30.

Directions: Find the average of each group of numbers. Draw a line from each problem to the correct average.

12 + 14 + 29 + 1 =   410

33 + 17 + 14 + 20 + 16 =   83

782 + 276 + 172 =   15

81 + 82 + 91 + 78 =   14

14 + 24 + 10 + 31 + 5 + 6 = 20

A baseball player had 3 hits in game one, 2 hits in game two, and 4 hits in game three. How many hits did she average over the three games? _____

Averaging

Directions: Find the averages.

Ted went bowling. He had scores of 112, 124, and 100. What was his average?

_____

The baseball team played 6 games. They had 12 hits, 6 hits, 18 hits, 36 hits, 11 hits, and 7 hits. What is the average number of hits in a game?

_____

In 3 games of football, Chris gained 156, 268, and 176 yards running. How many yards did he average in a game?

_____

Jane scored 18, 15, 26, and 21 points in 4 basketball games. How many points did she average?

_____

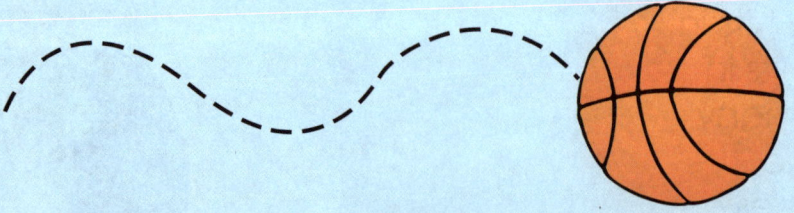

Averaging

Averaging can be used to keep track of your grades.

Example: Average the grades for each subject.

Sally has the following grades:
English — 75, 84, 95;
Spelling — 98, 92, 80;
Math — 80, 88, 95.

Her averages are:
English — 75 + 84 + 95 = 254 ÷ 3 = 84.7
Spelling — 98 + 92 + 80 = 270 ÷ 3 = 90.0
Math — 80 + 88 + 95 = 263 ÷ 3 = 87.7

Directions: Find the averages.

1. Write the number of minutes you do homework each night for a week. What is the average of those times?

_____

2. Keep track of the following for 1 week and find the average:

   a. Time spent watching TV _____

   b. Time spent playing video games _____

   c. Time spent on the computer _____

   d. Time spent doing chores _____

Review

Directions: Divide.

$3\overline{)268}$ $15\overline{)165}$

$27\overline{)489}$ $48\overline{)695}$ $79\overline{)937}$ $49\overline{)683}$

$91\overline{)848}$ $73\overline{)592}$ $59\overline{)473}$ $23\overline{)1,268}$

$67\overline{)2,543}$ $81\overline{)3,608}$ $37\overline{)8,432}$ $97\overline{)4,528}$

Directions: Find the averages.

22, 38   _____   105, 263, 331   _____

248, 325, 250, 69   _____   17, 18, 36, 28, 6   _____

Fractions

A **fraction** is a number that names part of a whole, such as $\frac{1}{2}$ or $\frac{1}{3}$.

A fraction is made up of two numbers—the **numerator** (top number) and the **denominator** (bottom number). The larger the denominator, the smaller each of the equal parts. $\frac{1}{16}$ is smaller than $\frac{1}{2}$.

Directions: Study the fractions below.

1 whole.

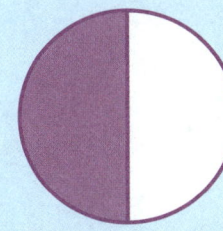

2 equal parts or halves

One-half of the circle is shaded. $\frac{1}{2}$

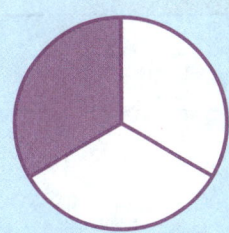

3 equal parts or thirds

One-third of the circle is shaded. $\frac{1}{3}$

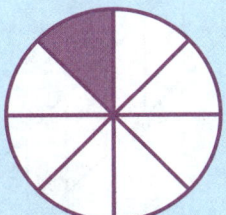

4 equal parts or halves

One-fourth of the circle is shaded. $\frac{1}{4}$

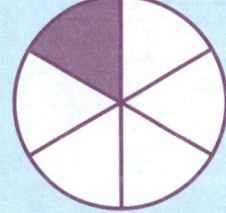

5 equal parts or fifths

One-fifth of the circle is shaded. $\frac{1}{5}$

6 equal parts or sixths

One-sixth of the circle is shaded. $\frac{1}{6}$

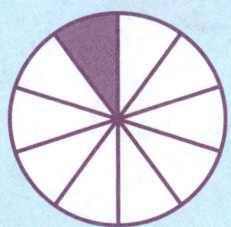

8 equal parts or eighths

One-eighth of the circle is shaded. $\frac{1}{8}$

10 equal parts or tenths

One-tenth of the circle is shaded. $\frac{1}{10}$

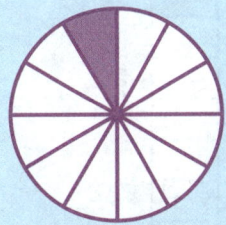

12 equal parts or twelfths

One-twelfth of the circle is shaded. $\frac{1}{12}$

Fractions

Directions: Name the fraction that is shaded.

Examples:

3 of 4 equal parts
are shaded.

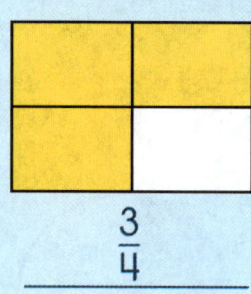

$\dfrac{3}{4}$

12 of 16 equal
parts are shaded.

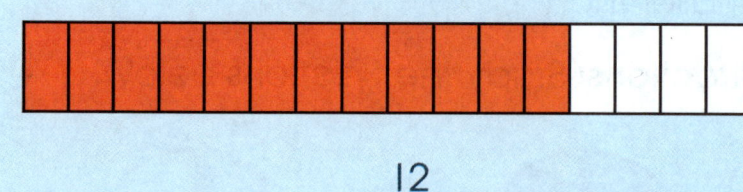

$\dfrac{12}{16}$

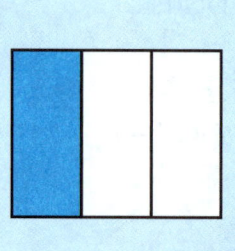

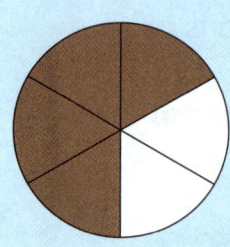

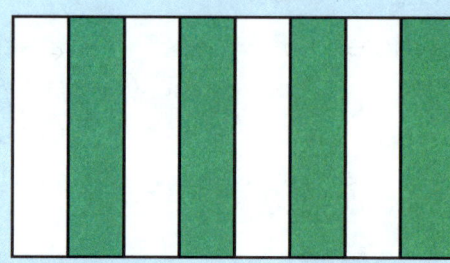

_____

_____

_____

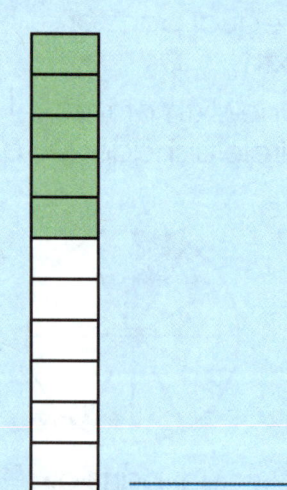

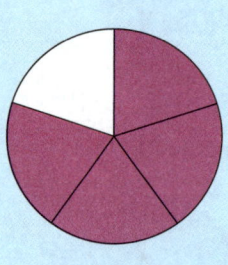

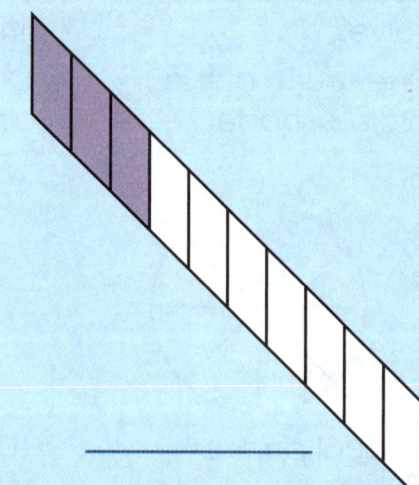

_____

_____

_____

Fraction Pieces

Directions: Cut apart the fraction pieces below. Use them to help you work with fractions. Store the fraction sets in separate plastic bags.

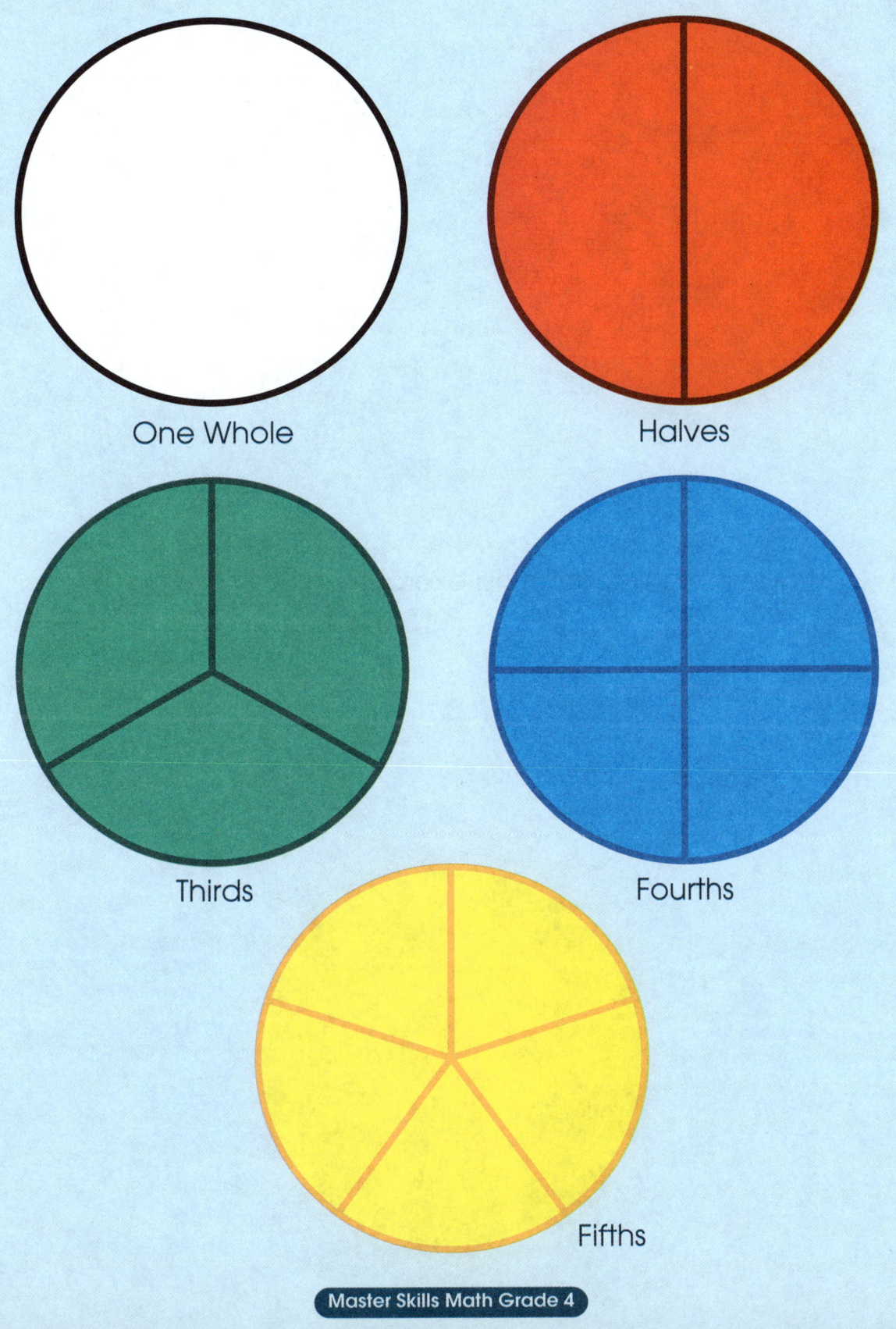

One Whole

Halves

Thirds

Fourths

Fifths

Page is blank for cutting exercise on previous page.

Fraction Pieces

Directions: Cut apart the fraction pieces below. Use them to help you work with fractions. Store the fraction sets in separate plastic bags.

Sixths

Eighths

Tenths

Twelfths

Sixteenths

Page is blank for cutting exercise on previous page.

When adding fractions with the same denominator, the denominator stays the same. Add only the numerators.

Example: numerator
            denominator $\frac{1}{8}$ + $\frac{2}{8}$ = $\frac{3}{8}$

Directions: Add the fractions on the flowers. Begin in the center of each flower and add each petal. The first one is done for you.

Example:

Fractions: Subtraction

When subtracting fractions with the same denominator, the denominator stays the same. Subtract only the numerators.

Directions: Solve the problems, working from left to right. As you find each answer, copy the letter from the key into the numbered blanks. The answer is the name of a famous American. The first one is done for you.

T $\frac{1}{8}$	P $\frac{5}{24}$	H $\frac{1}{4}$	F $\frac{4}{12}$	E $\frac{2}{7}$
J $\frac{3}{12}$	E $\frac{3}{9}$	O $\frac{2}{9}$	F $\frac{4}{8}$	R $\frac{7}{16}$
O $\frac{2}{8}$	Y $\frac{8}{20}$	Q $\frac{1}{32}$	M $\frac{1}{3}$	S $\frac{5}{20}$
A $\frac{1}{12}$	R $\frac{12}{15}$	S $\frac{3}{5}$	N $\frac{2}{6}$	O $\frac{11}{15}$

1. $\frac{3}{8} - \frac{2}{8} = \frac{1}{8}$
2. $\frac{2}{4} - \frac{1}{4} = $____
3. $\frac{5}{9} - \frac{3}{9} = $____
4. $\frac{2}{3} - \frac{1}{3} = $____
5. $\frac{8}{12} - \frac{7}{12} = $____

6. $\frac{4}{5} - \frac{1}{5} = $____
7. $\frac{6}{12} - \frac{3}{12} = $____
8. $\frac{4}{9} - \frac{1}{9} = $____
9. $\frac{11}{12} - \frac{7}{12} = $____
10. $\frac{7}{8} - \frac{3}{8} = $____

11. $\frac{4}{7} - \frac{2}{7} = $____
12. $\frac{14}{16} - \frac{7}{16} = $____
13. $\frac{18}{20} - \frac{13}{20} = $____
14. $\frac{13}{15} - \frac{2}{15} = $____
15. $\frac{5}{6} - \frac{3}{6} = $____

Who helped write the Declaration of Independence?

T __ __ __ __ __   __ __ __ __ __ __ __ __ __
1 2 3 4 5 6   7 8 9 10 11 12 13 14 15

Fractions: Mixed Numbers

A **mixed number** is a number written as a whole number and a fraction, such as $6\frac{5}{8}$.

To change a fraction into a mixed number, divide the denominator (bottom number) into the numerator (top number). Write the remainder over the denominator.

Example:

$$\frac{14}{6} = 2\frac{2}{6}$$

$$6)\overline{14} \quad \begin{array}{r} 2\ R2 \\ 14 \\ -12 \\ \hline 2 \end{array}$$

To change a mixed number into a fraction, multiply the denominator by the whole number, add the numerator, and write it on top of the denominator.

Example:

$$3\frac{1}{7} = \frac{22}{7} \quad (7 \times 3) + 1 = \frac{22}{7}$$

Directions: Write each fraction as a mixed number. Write each mixed number as a fraction.

$\frac{21}{6} = $ _____ $\frac{24}{5} = $ _____ $\frac{10}{3} = $ _____ $\frac{21}{4} = $ _____

$\frac{11}{6} = $ _____ $\frac{13}{4} = $ _____ $\frac{12}{5} = $ _____ $\frac{10}{9} = $ _____

$4\frac{3}{8} = \frac{\Box}{8}$ $2\frac{1}{3} = \frac{\Box}{3}$ $4\frac{3}{5} = \frac{\Box}{5}$ $3\frac{4}{6} = \frac{\Box}{6}$

$7\frac{1}{4} = \frac{\Box}{4}$ $2\frac{3}{5} = \frac{\Box}{5}$ $7\frac{1}{2} = \frac{\Box}{2}$ $6\frac{5}{7} = \frac{\Box}{7}$

$\frac{23}{7} = $ _____ $8\frac{1}{3} = $ _____ $9\frac{3}{7} = $ _____ $\frac{32}{24} = $ _____

Fractions: Adding Mixed Numbers

When adding mixed numbers, add the whole numbers first, then the fractions.

Examples:

$$\begin{array}{r} 9\frac{1}{3} \\ +3\frac{1}{3} \\ \hline 12\frac{2}{3} \end{array} \qquad \begin{array}{r} 2\frac{3}{6} \\ +1\frac{1}{6} \\ \hline 3\frac{4}{6} \end{array}$$

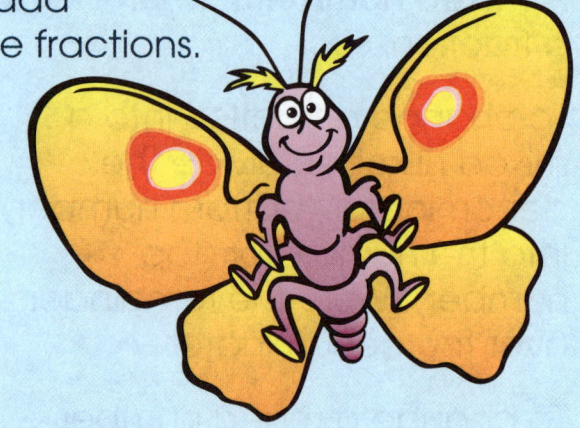

Directions: Add the number in the center to the number in each surrounding section.

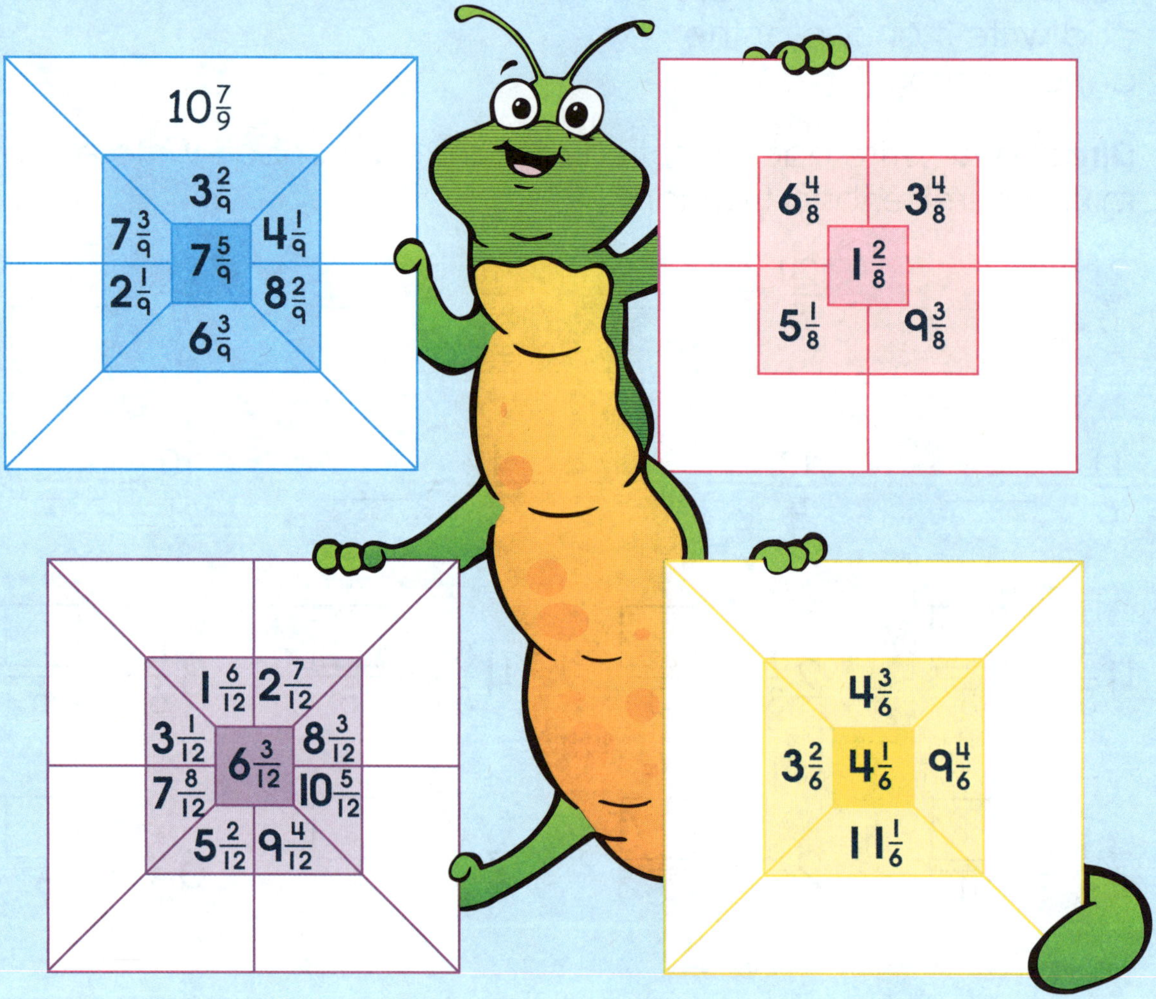
$10\frac{7}{9}$ $3\frac{2}{9}$ $7\frac{3}{9}$ $4\frac{1}{9}$ $7\frac{5}{9}$ $2\frac{1}{9}$ $8\frac{2}{9}$ $6\frac{3}{9}$
$6\frac{4}{8}$ $3\frac{4}{8}$ $1\frac{2}{8}$ $5\frac{1}{8}$ $9\frac{3}{8}$
$1\frac{6}{12}$ $2\frac{7}{12}$ $3\frac{1}{12}$ $8\frac{3}{12}$ $6\frac{3}{12}$ $7\frac{8}{12}$ $10\frac{5}{12}$ $5\frac{2}{12}$ $9\frac{4}{12}$
$4\frac{3}{6}$ $3\frac{2}{6}$ $4\frac{1}{6}$ $9\frac{4}{6}$ $11\frac{1}{6}$

When subtracting mixed numbers, subtract the fractions first, then the whole numbers.

Directions: Subtract the mixed numbers. The first one is done for you.

$$7\frac{3}{8} \quad 4\frac{5}{6} \quad 4\frac{1}{2} \quad 7\frac{5}{8} \quad 6\frac{6}{8} \quad 5\frac{3}{4}$$
$$-4\frac{2}{8} \quad -3\frac{1}{6} \quad -3 \quad -6\frac{3}{8} \quad -1\frac{1}{8} \quad -1\frac{1}{4}$$
$$3\frac{1}{8}$$

$$5\frac{2}{3} \quad 4\frac{8}{10} \quad 9\frac{8}{9} \quad 7\frac{2}{3} \quad 7\frac{2}{3} \quad 9\frac{8}{10}$$
$$-3\frac{1}{3} \quad -3\frac{3}{10} \quad -4\frac{3}{9} \quad -6\frac{1}{3} \quad -5 \quad -6\frac{3}{10}$$

Sally needs $1\frac{3}{8}$ yards of cloth to make a dress. She has $4\frac{5}{8}$ yards. How much cloth will be left over? _____

Equivalent Fractions

Equivalent fractions are two different fractions that represent the same number. **Example:**  $\frac{1}{2}$ = 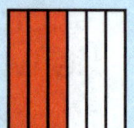 $\frac{3}{6}$

Directions: Complete these equivalent fractions. Use your fraction pieces from pages 53 and 55.

$$\frac{1}{3} = \frac{}{6} \qquad \frac{1}{2} = \frac{}{4} \qquad \frac{3}{4} = \frac{}{8} \qquad \frac{1}{3} = \frac{}{9}$$

Directions: Write the fraction for the shaded area under each figure. Circle the figure that shows a fraction equivalent to figure a.

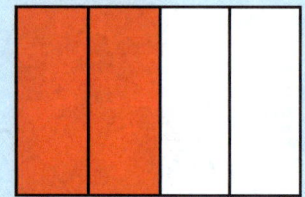

a. _____

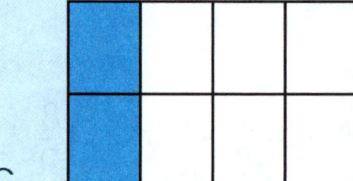

c. _____

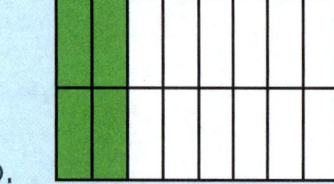

b. _____

d. _____

To find an equivalent fraction, multiply both parts of the fraction by the same number.

Example: $\frac{2}{3} \times \frac{3}{3} = \frac{6}{9}$

Directions: Find an equivalent fraction.

$$\frac{1}{4} = \frac{}{8} \qquad \frac{3}{4} = \frac{}{16} \qquad \frac{4}{5} = \frac{8}{} \qquad \frac{3}{8} = \frac{}{24}$$

Reducing Fractions

Reducing a fraction means finding the greatest common factor and divide.

Example: $\frac{5}{15}$ factors of 5: 1, 5

factors of 15: 1, 3, 5, 15

5 is the greatest common factor. Divide both the numerator and denominator by 5.

$5 \div 5 = 1$
$15 \div 5 = 3$

Directions: Reduce each fraction. Circle the correct answer.

$\frac{2}{4} = \frac{1}{2}, \frac{1}{6}, \frac{1}{8}$ $\frac{3}{9} = \frac{1}{6}, \frac{1}{3}, \frac{3}{6}$ $\frac{5}{10} = \frac{1}{5}, \frac{1}{2}, \frac{5}{6}$

$\frac{4}{12} = \frac{1}{4}, \frac{1}{3}, \frac{2}{3}$ $\frac{10}{15} = \frac{2}{3}, \frac{2}{5}, \frac{2}{7}$

Directions: Find the way home. Color the boxes with fractions equivalent to $\frac{1}{8}$ or $\frac{1}{3}$.

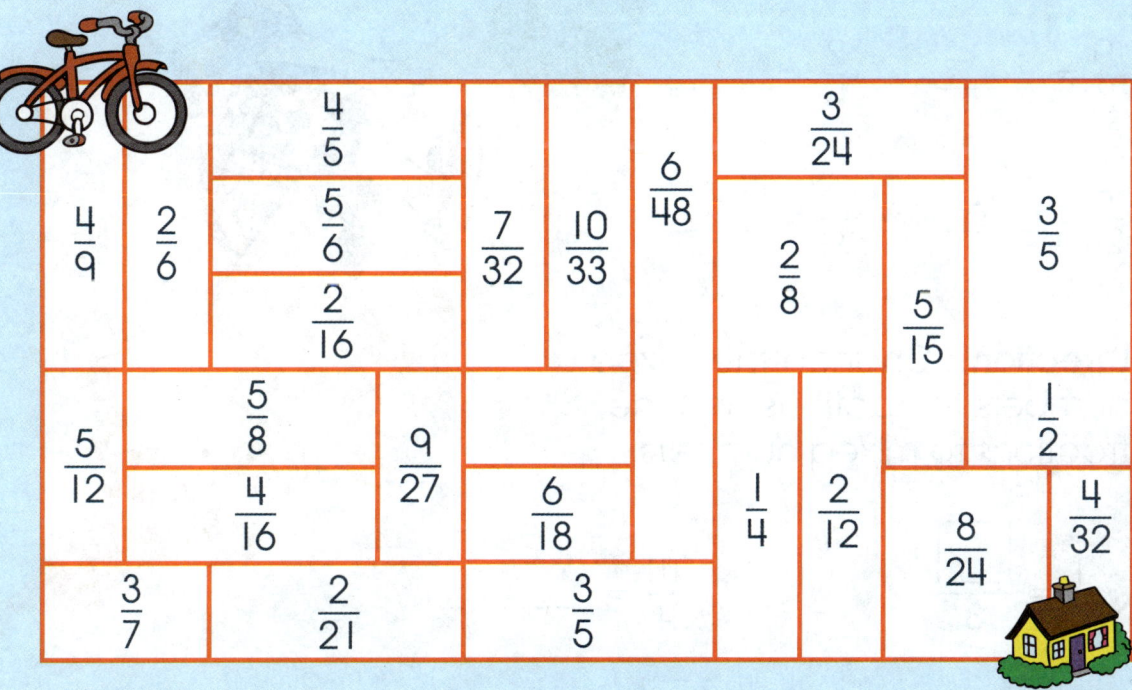

Review

Directions: Add or subtract the fractions and mixed numbers.

$$4\frac{7}{8}$$
$$-2\frac{5}{8}$$

$$8\frac{3}{9}$$
$$+2\frac{5}{9}$$

$$3\frac{1}{8}$$
$$+1\frac{3}{8}$$

$$4\frac{5}{6}$$
$$-3\frac{1}{6}$$

$$7\frac{5}{11}$$
$$+3\frac{3}{11}$$

$\frac{4}{12} + \frac{3}{12} =$ _____

$\frac{3}{5} + \frac{1}{5} =$ _____

$\frac{3}{8} - \frac{1}{8} =$ _____

$\frac{3}{4} - \frac{2}{4} =$ _____

Directions:
Reduce the fractions.

$\frac{4}{6} =$ _____

$\frac{7}{21} =$ _____

$\frac{9}{12} =$ _____

$\frac{2}{4} =$ _____

$\frac{6}{24} =$ _____

$\frac{8}{32} =$ _____

Directions: Change the mixed numbers to fractions and the fractions to mixed numbers.

$3\frac{1}{3} = \dfrac{\boxed{}}{3}$

$\frac{14}{4} =$ _____

$\frac{26}{6} =$ _____

$3\frac{7}{12} = \dfrac{\boxed{}}{12}$

Fractions to Decimals

When a figure is divided into 10 equal parts, the parts are called tenths. Tenths can be written two ways—as a fraction or a decimal. A **decimal** is a number with one or more places to the right of a decimal point, such as 6.5 or 2.25. A **decimal point** is the dot between the ones place and the tenths place.

Examples:

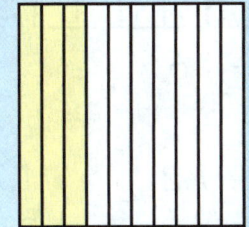

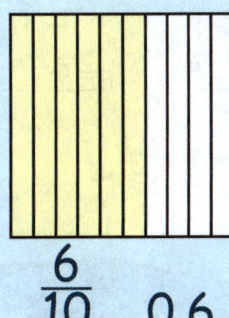

$\frac{3}{10}$ or 0.3 of the square is shaded.

Directions: Write the decimal and fraction for the shaded parts of the following figures. The first one is done for you.

$\frac{6}{10}$ 0.6

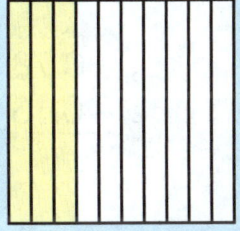 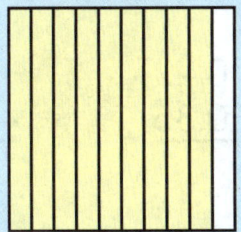 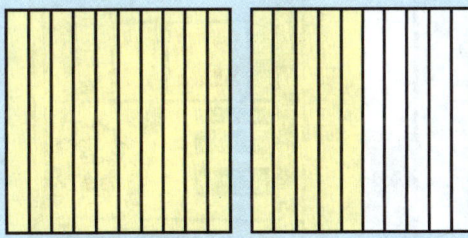

____ ____   ____ ____   ____ ____

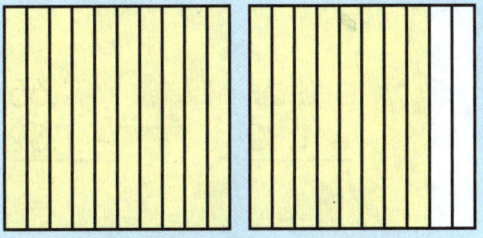 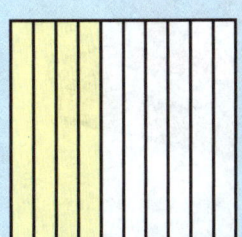 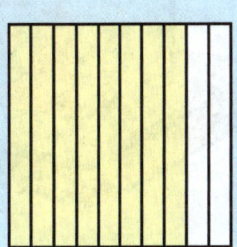

____ ____   ____ ____   ____ ____

Decimals

Directions: Add or subtract. Remember to include the decimal point in your answers.

Example:

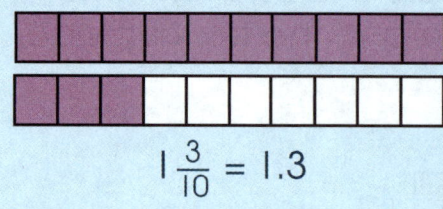

$1\frac{3}{10} = 1.3$

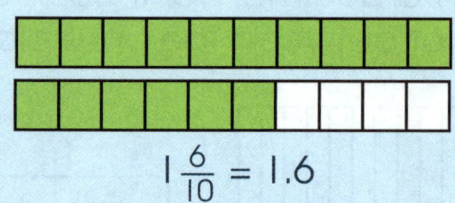

$1\frac{6}{10} = 1.6$

$$\begin{array}{r} 1.3 \\ + 1.6 \\ \hline 2.9 \end{array}$$

8.1 + 1.7	4.1 + 6.2	0.5 + 1.6	7.6 − 6.5	7.2 − 2.6	1.2 + 5.0	8.7 − 3.9

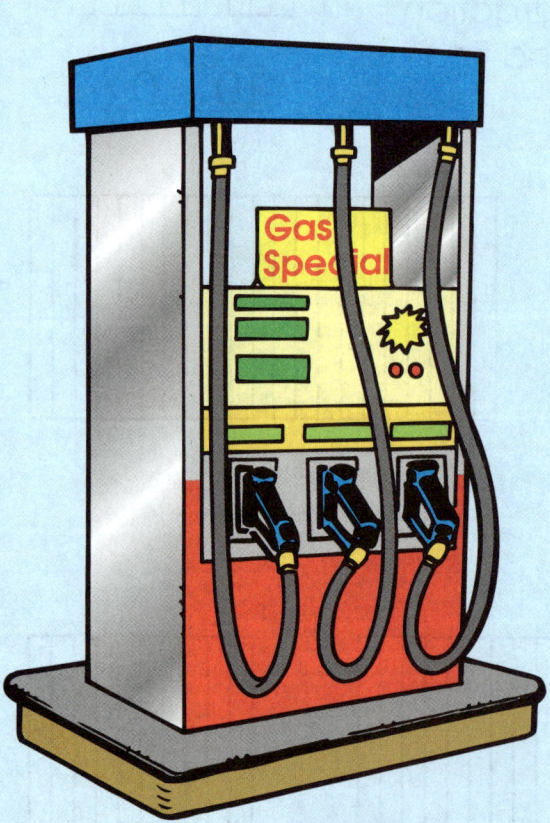

$$\begin{array}{r} 7.8 \\ - 6.8 \\ \hline \end{array} \qquad \begin{array}{r} 16.5 \\ - 7.3 \\ \hline \end{array} \qquad \begin{array}{r} 6.4 \\ + 5.3 \\ \hline \end{array}$$

$$\begin{array}{r} 0.42 \\ + 0.35 \\ \hline \end{array} \qquad \begin{array}{r} 0.98 \\ - 0.87 \\ \hline \end{array} \qquad \begin{array}{r} 0.78 \\ - 0.13 \\ \hline \end{array}$$

$$\begin{array}{r} 0.95 \\ - 0.14 \\ \hline \end{array} \qquad \begin{array}{r} 3.23 \\ + 2.48 \\ \hline \end{array} \qquad \begin{array}{r} 4.68 \\ - 2.65 \\ \hline \end{array}$$

$$\begin{array}{r} 6.98 \\ + 1.40 \\ \hline \end{array} \qquad \begin{array}{r} 3.27 \\ + 1.82 \\ \hline \end{array} \qquad \begin{array}{r} 4.65 \\ - 1.32 \\ \hline \end{array}$$

Mr. Martin went on a car trip with his family. Mr. Martin purchased gas 3 times. He bought 6.7 gallons, 7.3 gallons, then 5.8 gallons of gas. How much gas did he purchase in all? _____

Decimals: Hundredths

The next smallest decimal unit after a tenth is called a hundredth. One hundredth is one unit of a figure divided into 100 units. Written as a decimal, it is one digit to the right of the tenths place.

Examples:

One square divided into hundredths, 34 hundredths are shaded. Write: 0.34.

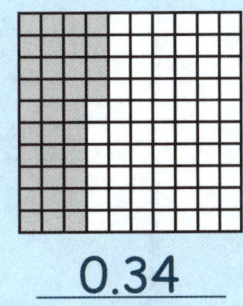

ones	tenths	hundredths
0	3	4

0.34

Directions: Write the decimal for the shaded parts of the following figures.

 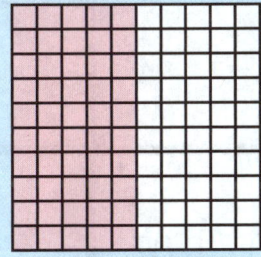 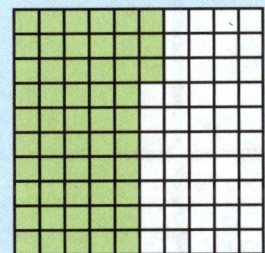 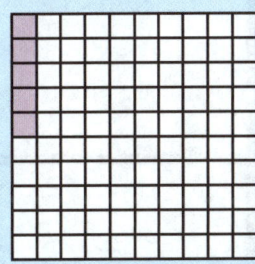

_____ _____ _____ _____

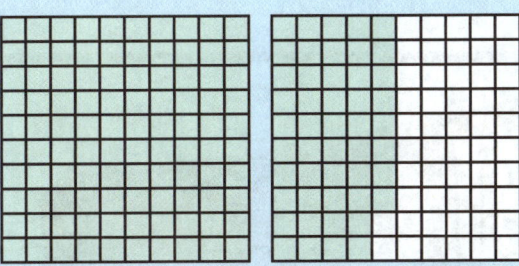 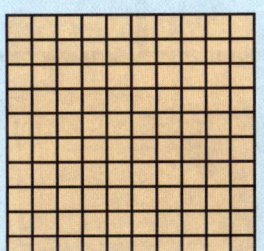 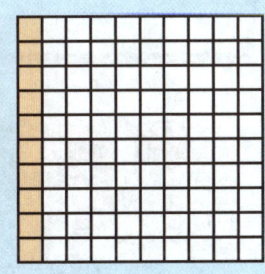

_____ _____

Directions: Add or subtract the problems. Then, fill in the circle next to the correct answer.

Example:

2.4
+ 1.7

○ 2.5
○ 3.1
● 4.1

2.8 + 3.4 ○ 5.2 ○ 7.4 ○ 6.2	5.7 − 3.8 ○ 1.9 ○ 2.5 ○ 2.9	7.6 + 8.9 ○ 15.9 ○ 16.5 ○ 17.3
16.3 + 9.8 ○ 25.11 ○ 26.1 ○ 26.01	28.6 + 43.9 ○ 73.6 ○ 72.5 ○ 71.9	43.9 + 56.5 ○ 100.4 ○ 107.4 ○ 101.4
11.57 + 10.64 ○ 22.21 ○ 1.93 ○ 21.12	27.83 − 14.94 ○ 14.09 ○ 12.89 ○ 11.97	106.935 − 95.824 ○ 111.1 ○ 111.11 ○ 11.111

The high-speed train traveled 87.90 miles on day one, 127.86 miles on day two, and 113.41 miles on day three. How many miles did it travel in all? _____

Fractions and Decimals

Directions: Compare the fraction to the decimal in each box. Circle the larger number.

Example:

fourths

tenths

$\frac{1}{4}$ 0.1

$\frac{2}{4}$ 0.2	$\frac{3}{4}$ 0.3	$\frac{1}{2}$ 0.6	$\frac{1}{4}$ 0.4
$\frac{1}{3}$ 0.1	$\frac{1}{4}$ 0.7	$\frac{2}{4}$ 0.8	$\frac{3}{4}$ 0.9
$\frac{5}{6}$ 0.5	$\frac{2}{5}$ 0.6	$\frac{3}{12}$ 0.9	$\frac{1}{6}$ 0.2
$\frac{2}{3}$ 0.8	$\frac{1}{5}$ 0.3	$\frac{2}{5}$ 0.7	$\frac{3}{10}$ 0.5

Identifying Operations

Directions: Write the correct operation sign (+, −, x, ÷) in each circle to correctly complete the problem. The first two are done for you.

5 $\times$ 6 = 30	0.3 $-$ 0.2 = 0.1	128 ◯ 56 = 72
4 ◯ 8 = 32	$1\frac{2}{6}$ ◯ $2\frac{3}{6}$ = $3\frac{5}{6}$	49 ◯ 7 = 7
54 ◯ 6 = 9	$\frac{1}{10}$ ◯ $\frac{4}{10}$ = $\frac{5}{10}$	188 ◯ 21 = 209
28 ◯ 16 = 44	$3\frac{3}{8}$ ◯ $2\frac{2}{8}$ = $1\frac{1}{8}$	16 ◯ 4 = 4
63 ◯ 7 = 9	12 ◯ 12 = 144	10 ◯ 0 = 0
49 ◯ 9 = 40	100 ◯ 5 = 20	0.91 ◯ 0.81 = 0.1
48 ◯ 12 = 4	98 ◯ 43 = 55	0.3 ◯ 0.3 = 0.6
39 ◯ 19 = 20	0.9 ◯ 0.7 = 0.2	0.5 ◯ 0.5 = 1.0
72 ◯ 8 = 9	1.68 ◯ 0.9 = 0.78	0.97 ◯ .50 = 1.47

Directions: Solve the problems. Circle the letter with the correct answer. Write the letters in order to read the message.

1.	$348 - 227 =$	121	(M)	425	S
2.	$542 \times 6 =$	5,683	W	3,252	A
3.	$328 + 593 =$	921	T	149	N
4.	$1,280 \div 40 =$	92	L	32	H
5.	$24 \times 52 =$	2,386	W	1,248	I
6.	$863 - 438 =$	425	S	234	U
7.	$4,586 + 1,097 =$	3,489	Q	5,683	W
8.	$480 \div 4 =$	32	H	120	O
9.	$0.5 + 0.9 =$	1.4	N	0.14	E
10.	$1.6 - 0.9 =$	0.7	D	0.9	T
11.	$3\frac{1}{5} + 2\frac{3}{5}$	$5\frac{4}{5}$	E	$4\frac{2}{5}$	L
12.	$\frac{4}{8} - \frac{1}{4}$	$\frac{3}{8}$	Y	$\frac{1}{4}$	R
13.	$2,193 - 1,864 =$	329	F	591	Y
14.	$26 \times 9 =$	234	U	744	L
15.	$42 \div 6 =$	8	M	7	L

$\underline{\text{M}}_{1}$ $\underline{\hphantom{M}}_{2}$ $\underline{\hphantom{M}}_{3}$ $\underline{\hphantom{M}}_{4}$ $\underline{\hphantom{M}}_{5}$ $\underline{\hphantom{M}}_{6}$

$\underline{\hphantom{M}}_{7}$ $\underline{\hphantom{M}}_{8}$ $\underline{\hphantom{M}}_{9}$ $\underline{\hphantom{M}}_{10}$ $\underline{\hphantom{M}}_{11}$ $\underline{\hphantom{M}}_{12}$ $\underline{\hphantom{M}}_{13}$ $\underline{\hphantom{M}}_{14}$ $\underline{\hphantom{M}}_{15}$!

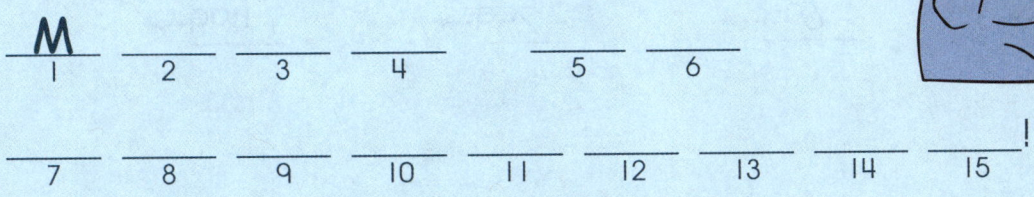

Review

Directions: Add or subtract to find the answers.

Bill jumped 28.5 feet. Jim jumped 27.3 feet.
How much farther did Bill jump than Jim? _____

Sue threw the discus 86.4 feet. Julie threw
the discus 93.8 feet. How much farther did
Julie throw the discus than Sue? _____

Kim, Monica, and Kelly swam
on the same team in the
butterfly relay race. Their
individual times were 32.8
seconds, 29.9 seconds, and
31.7 seconds. The winning
team's time was 93.5
seconds. Did Kim, Monica,
and Kelly swim the fastest
race? _____

Jake's times for the 100-meter
dash were 10.1 seconds, 12.5
seconds, and 11.8 seconds.
What was his total time? _____

Directions: Decide which sign is correct for each problem:
+, −, x, or ÷. Write it in the circle.

5 ◯ 5 = 25   100 ◯ 25 = 4   42 ◯ 38 = 80

152 ◯ 38 = 114   72 ◯ 12 = 6   9 ◯ 5 = 45

Directions: Round the numbers, then estimate each answer.

592 →   802 →   499 →   612 →
+ 312 →   − 695 →   − 299 →   + 499 →

Measurement: Inches

An **inch** is a unit of length in the standard system equal to $\frac{1}{12}$ of a foot. A ruler is used to measure inches.

This illustration shows a ruler measuring a 4-inch pencil, which can be written as 4" or 4 in.

Directions: Use a ruler to measure each object to the nearest inch.

1. The length of your foot _____

2. The width of your hand _____

3. The length of this page _____

4. The width of this page _____

5. The length of a large paper clip _____

6. The length of your toothbrush _____

7. The length of a comb _____

8. The height of a juice glass _____

9. The length of a fork _____

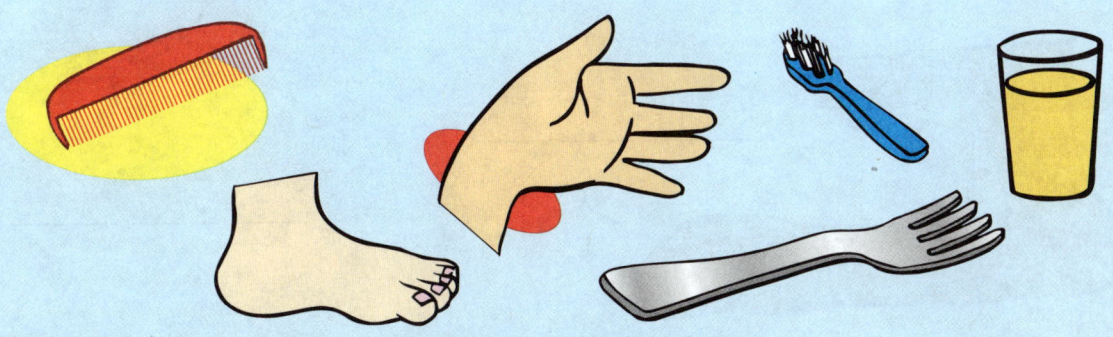

Directions: Use a ruler to measure the width of each foot to the nearest inch.

An inch is divided into smaller units, or fractions of an inch.

Example: This stick of gum is $2\frac{3}{4}$ inches long.

Directions: Use a ruler to measure each line to the nearest quarter of an inch. The first one is done for you.

1. $\frac{3}{4}$ inch _____

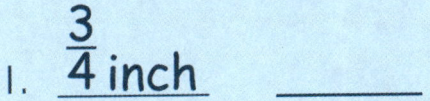

2. _____   _____

3. _____   _____

4. _____   _____

5. _____   _____

6. _____   _____

7. _____   _____

Directions: Use a ruler to measure to the nearest quarter of an inch.

How far did the grasshopper jump?

_____ + _____ + _____ + _____ = _____

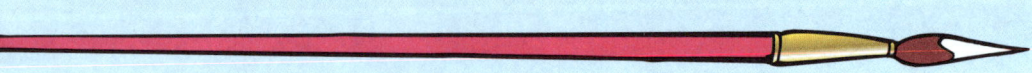

What is the total length of the paintbrushes?

_____ + _____ + _____ + _____ + _____ = _____

Measurement: Foot, Yard, Mile

Directions: Choose the measure of distance you would use for each object.

1 foot = 12 inches
1 yard = 3 feet
1 mile = 1,760 yards or 5,280 feet

_____ inches

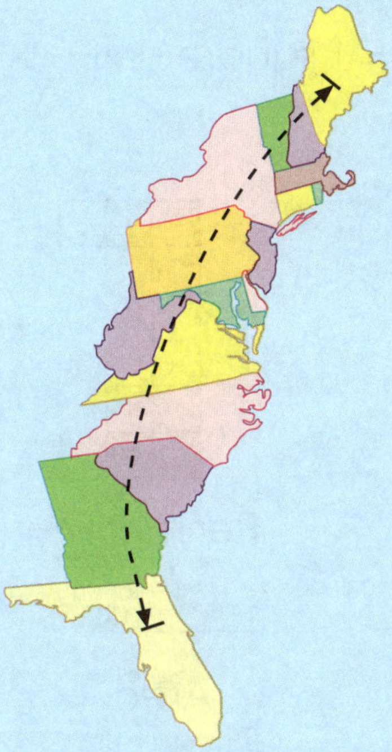

_____

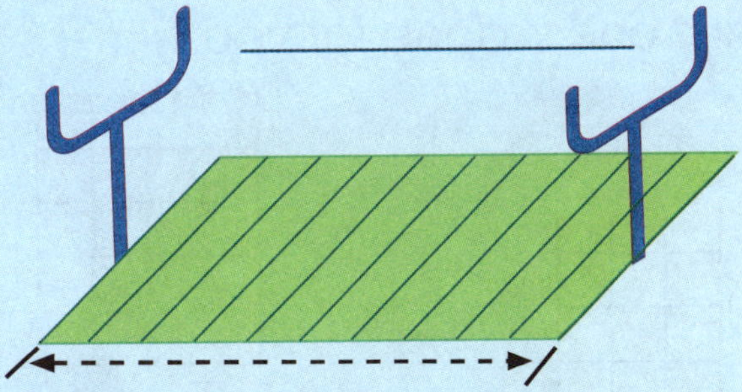

_____

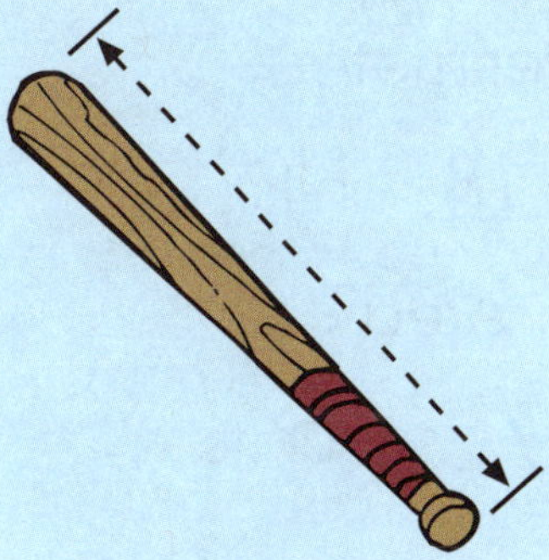

_____

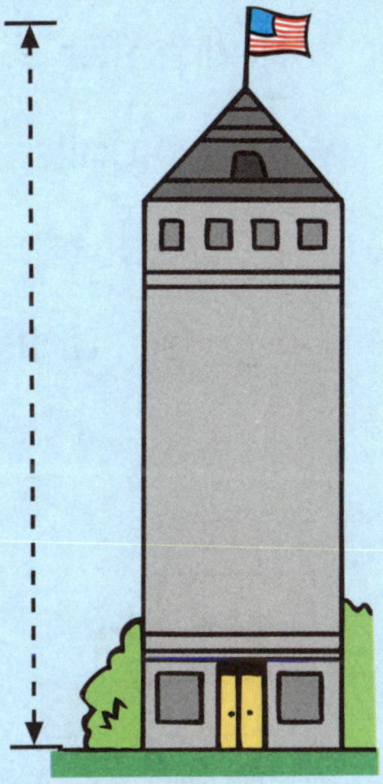

_____

_____

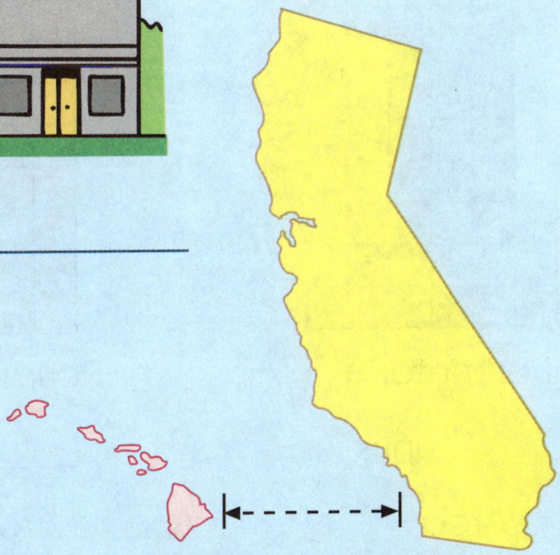

_____   _____

Perimeter is the distance around a figure. It is found by adding the lengths of the sides. **Area** is the number of square units needed to cover a region. The area is found by adding the number of square units. A unit can be any unit of measure. Most often inches, feet, or yards are used.

Directions: Find the perimeter and area for each figure. The first one is done for you.

□ = I square unit

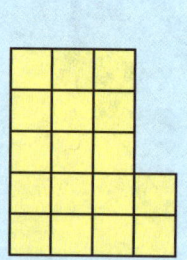

Perimeter =

__18__ units

Area =

__17__ sq. units

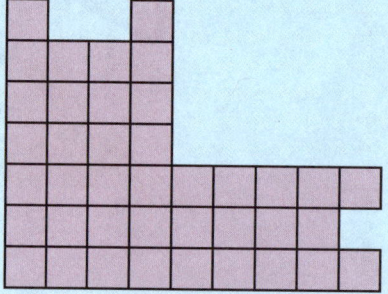

Perimeter =

_____ units

Area =

_____ sq. units

Perimeter =

_____ units

Area =

_____ sq. units

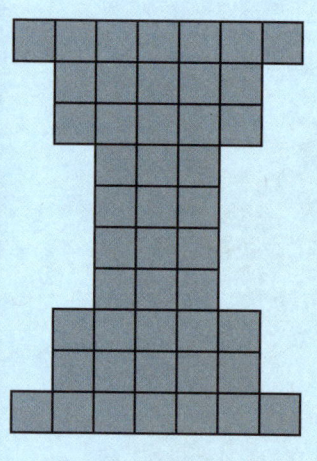

Perimeter =

_____ units

Area =

_____ sq. units

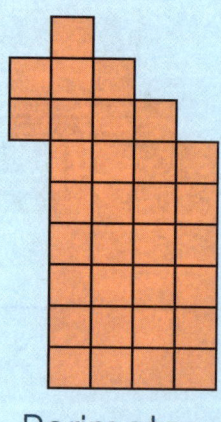

Perimeter =

_____ units

Area =

_____ sq. units

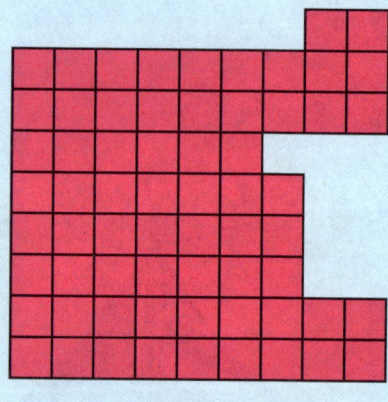

Perimeter =

_____ units

Area =

_____ sq. units

Measurement: Perimeter

Perimeter is calculated by adding the lengths of the sides of a figure.

Examples:

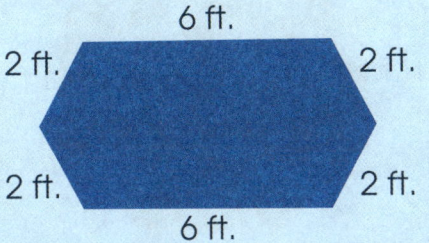

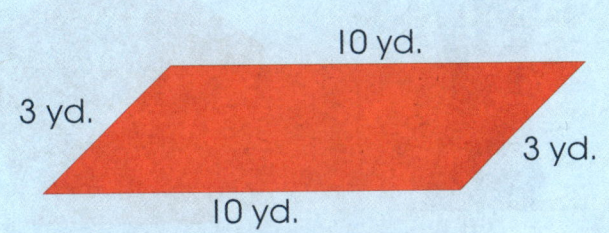

2 + 2 + 2 + 2 + 6 + 6 = 20
The perimeter of this
hexagon is 20 ft.

10 + 10 + 3 + 3 = 26
The perimeter of this
parallelogram is 26 yd.

Directions: Find the perimeter of the following figures.

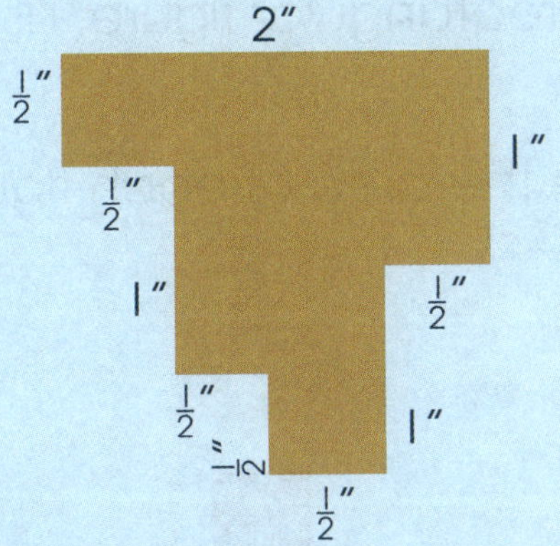

_____
Perimeter

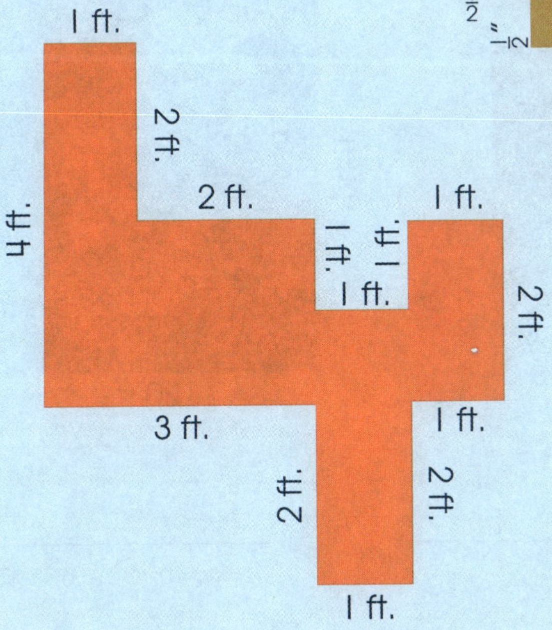

_____
Perimeter

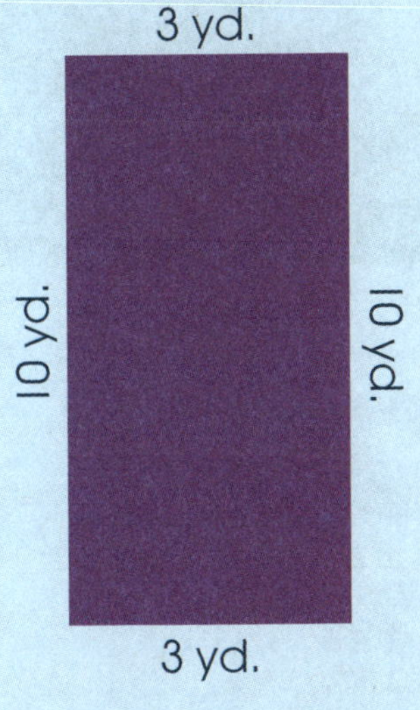

_____
Perimeter

Directions: Calculate the perimeter of each figure.

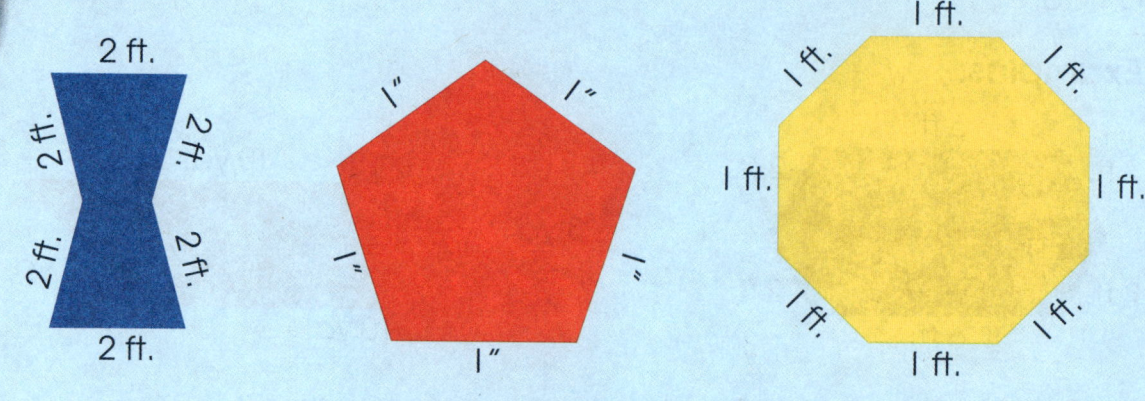

_____   _____   _____

Area is also calculated by multiplying the length times the width of a square or rectangular figure. Use the formula: A = l x w.

Directions: Calculate the area of each figure.

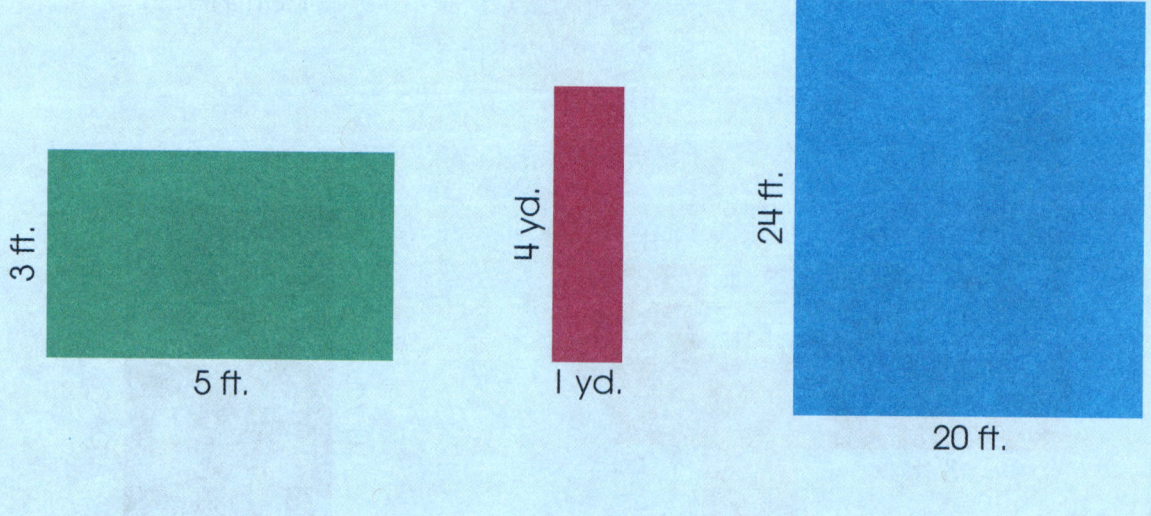

_____   _____   _____

Measurement: Volume

Volume is the number of cubic units that fit inside a figure.

Directions: Find the volume of each figure. The first one is done for you.

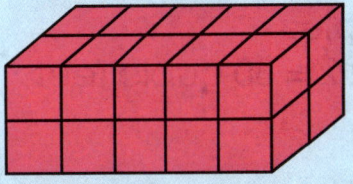

___4___ cubic units

_____ cubic units

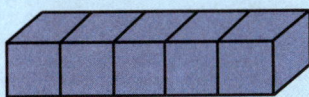

_____ cubic units

_____ cubic units

_____ cubic units

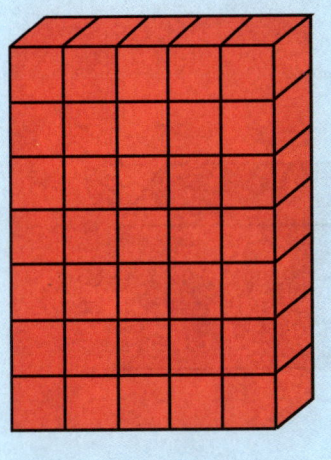

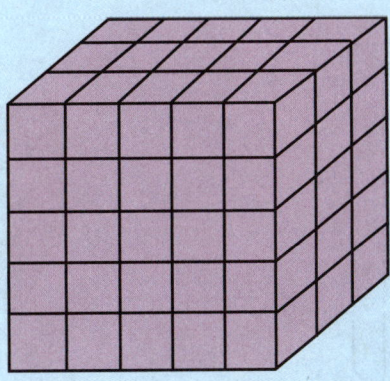

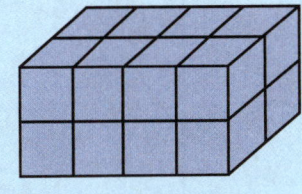

_____ cubic units

_____ cubic units

_____ cubic units

Measurement: Volume

The volume of a figure can also be calculated by multiplying the length times the width times the height. Use the formula: l x w x h.

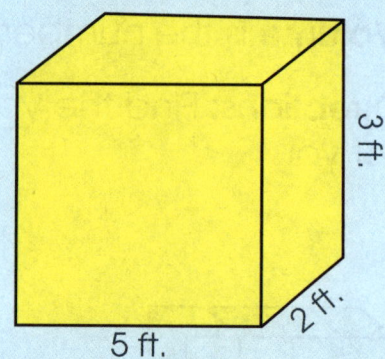

Example:
3 x 5 x 2 = 30 cubic feet

Directions: Find the volume of the following figures. Label your answers in feet, inches, or yards. The first one is done for you.

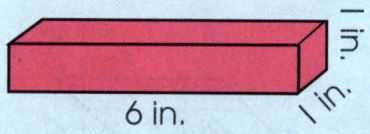

6 in. 1 in. 1 in.

<u>6 cubic inches</u>

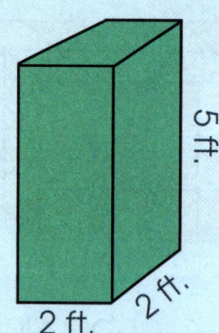

5 ft. 2 ft. 2 ft.

_____

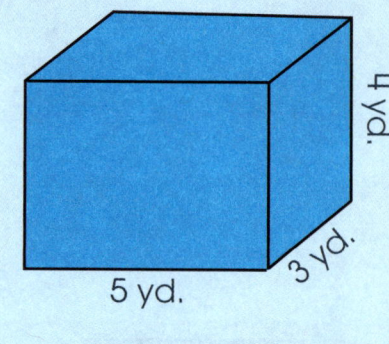

4 yd. 5 yd. 3 yd.

_____

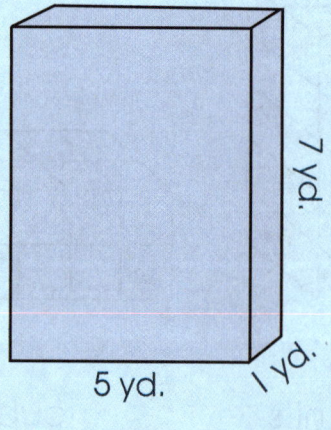

7 yd. 5 yd. 1 yd.

_____

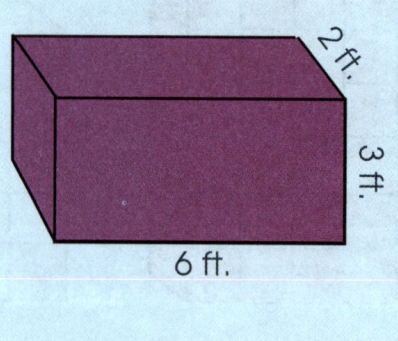

2 ft. 3 ft. 6 ft.

_____

The **cup**, **pint**, **quart**, and **gallon**, are units in the standard system for measuring liquids.

Directions: Gather the following materials: 2 dish tubs, one filled with water, sand, or rice; measuring cups; pint container; quart container; gallon container. Then, answer the questions and complete the chart.

1. Use the cup measure to pour water, sand, or rice into the pint container. How many cups did it take?

    _____ cups = 1 pint

2. Use the cup measure to find out how many cups are in a quart and a gallon.

    _____ cups = 1 quart

    _____ cups = 1 gallon

3. Use the pint container to pour water, sand, or rice into the quart container. How many pints are in a quart?

    _____ pints = 1 quart

4. How many pints does it take to fill a gallon?

    _____ pints = 1 gallon

5. Use the quart measure to find out how many quarts are in a gallon.

    _____ quarts = 1 gallon

Measurement Chart

_____ cups = 1 pint   _____ pints = 1 quart

_____ cups = 1 quart   _____ pints = 1 gallon

_____ cups = 1 gallon   _____ quarts = 1 gallon

Measurement: Cup, Pint, Quart, Gallon

Directions: Circle the number of objects to the right that equal the objects on the left. The first one is done for you.

2 cups = 1 pint   2 pints = 1 quart   4 quarts = 1 gallon

= 1 cup

= 1 pint   = 1 quart   = 1 gallon

The **ounce**, **pound**, and **ton** are units in the standard system for measuring weight.

ounce

pound

ton

16 ounces = 1 pound   2,000 pounds = 1 ton

Directions: Choose the measure of weight you would use for each object.

Example:  <u>ounces</u>

_____

_____

_____

_____

_____

_____

_____

Review

Directions: Find the perimeter and area of each figure.

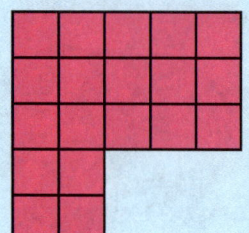

☐ = I square unit

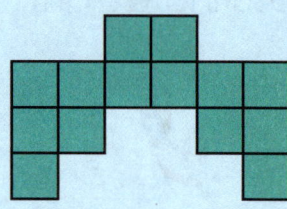

Perimeter = _____ units

Area = _____ sq. units

Perimeter = _____ units

Area = _____ sq. units

Directions: How much does it equal?

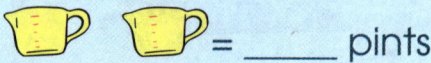 = _____ pints

 = _____ pints

Directions: Write whether you would use ounce, pound, or ton to weigh the following.

_____   _____   _____

Directions: Write whether you would use an inch, foot, yard, or mile to measure the following.

      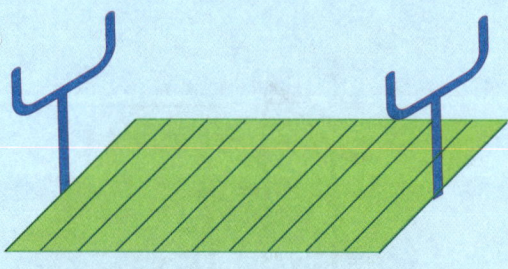

_____   _____   _____

In the metric system, there are three units of linear measurement: centimeter (cm), meter (m), and kilometer (km).

Centimeters (cm) are used to measure the lengths of small to medium-sized objects. **Meters (m)** measure the lengths of longer objects, such as the width of a swimming pool or height of a tree (100 cm = 1 meter). **Kilometers (km)** measure long distances, such as the distance from Cleveland to Cincinnati or the width of the Atlantic Ocean (1,000 m = 1 km).

Directions: Write whether you would use cm, m, or km to measure each object.

Chicago

New York City

Metric Measurement: Centimeter

Directions: Use a centimeter ruler to measure the width of each foot to the nearest centimeter.

A meter is a little longer than a yard—39.37 inches (a yard is 36 inches). A kilometer is equal to about $\frac{5}{8}$ of a mile.

Directions: Choose the measure of distance you would use for the following.

meter

_____

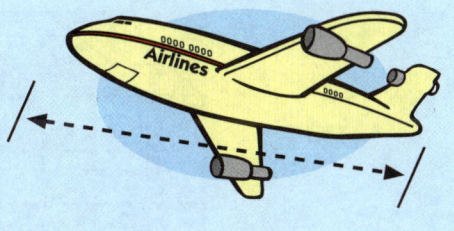

_____

_____

_____

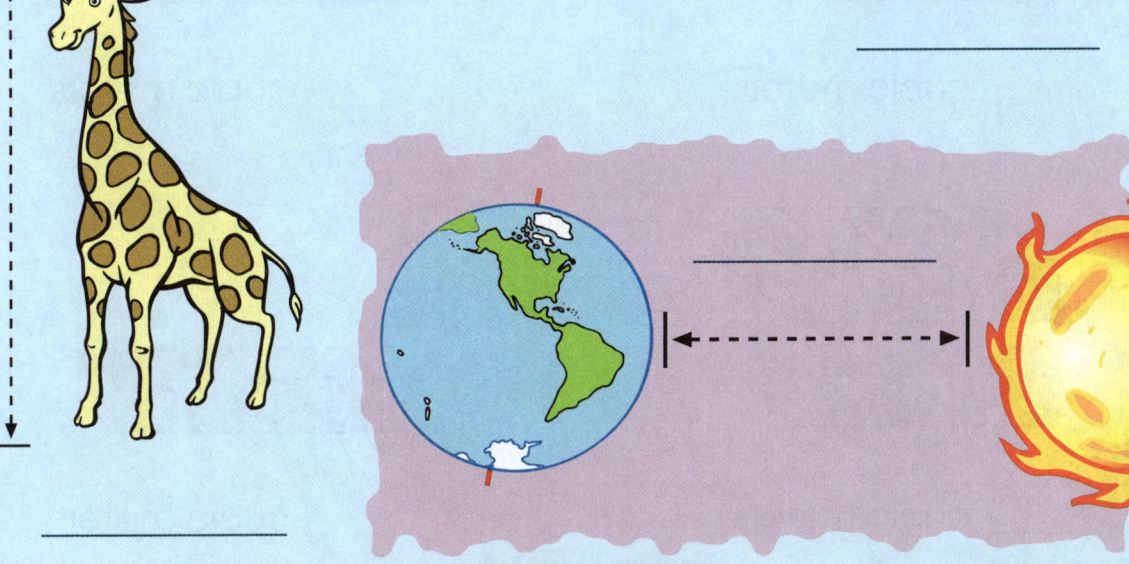

_____

_____

Metric Measurement: Perimeter, Area, Volume

Directions: Find the perimeter and area of each figure.

☐ = I square unit

Perimeter = _____ units

Area = _____ sq. units

Perimeter = _____ units

Area = _____ sq. units

Directions: Find the volume of each figure.

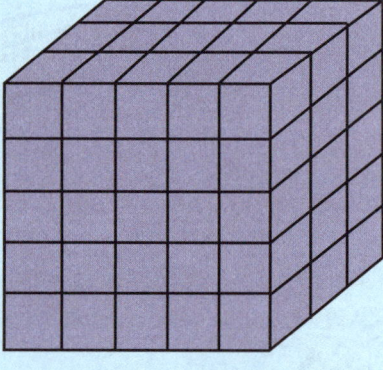

_____ cubic meters

_____ cubic meters

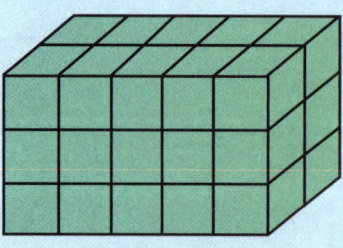

_____ cubic meters

_____ cubic meters

Metric Measurement: Perimeter

Directions: Calculate the perimeter of each figure.

Example:

4 + 5 + 4 + 1 + 2 + 3 + 2 = 21 meters

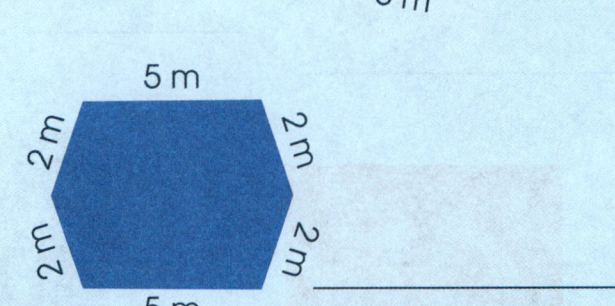

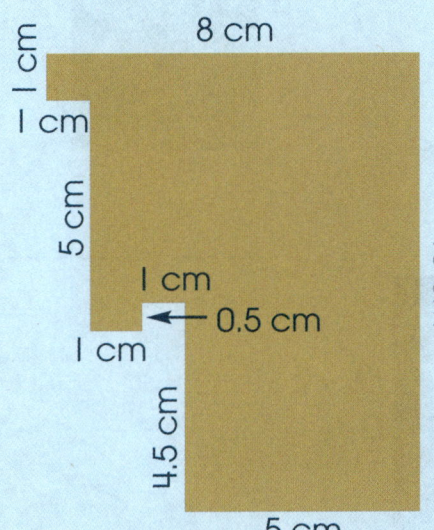

_____

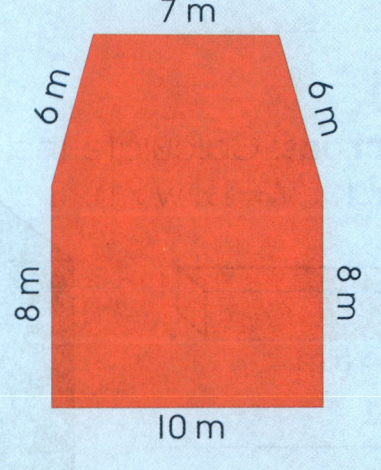

_____

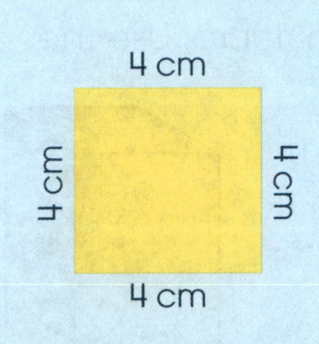

_____

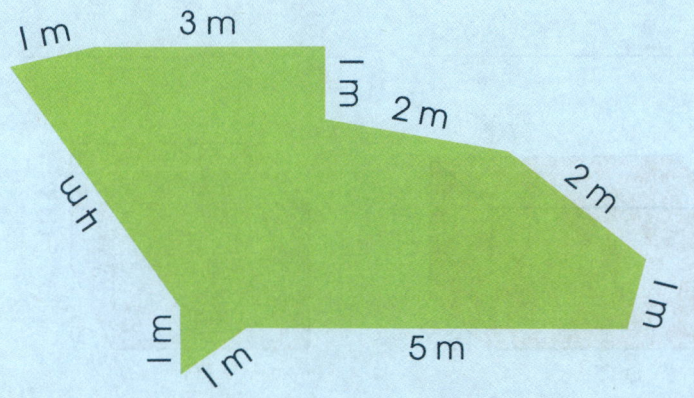

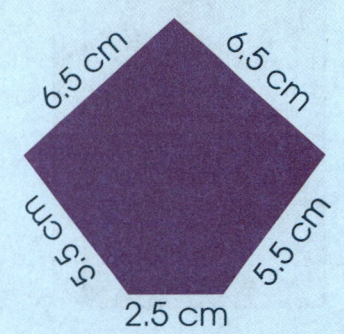

_____   _____

Directions: Calculate the area of each figure.

Use the formula: A = l x w.

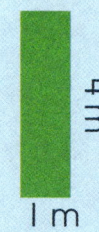
4 m
1 m

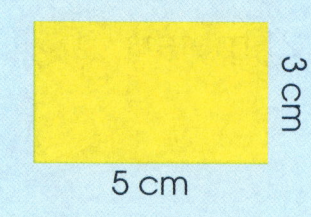
3 cm
5 cm

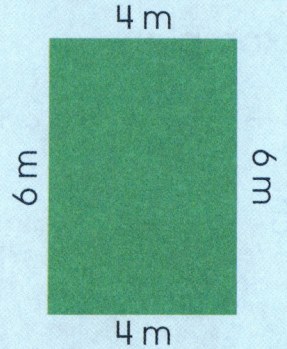
4 m
6 m
9 m
4 m

_____

_____

_____

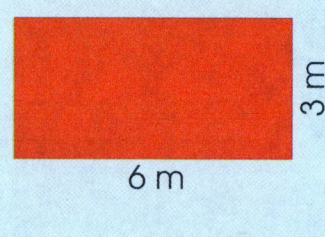
3 m
6 m

24 cm
20 cm

_____

_____

Directions: Calculate the volume of each figure. Use the formula: V = l x w x h.

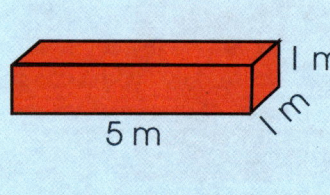
1 m
1 m
5 m

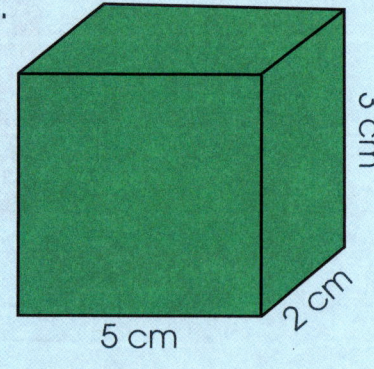
3 cm
5 cm
2 cm

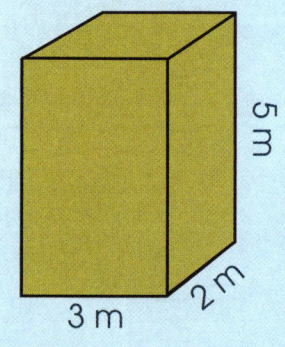
5 m
3 m
2 m

_____

_____

_____

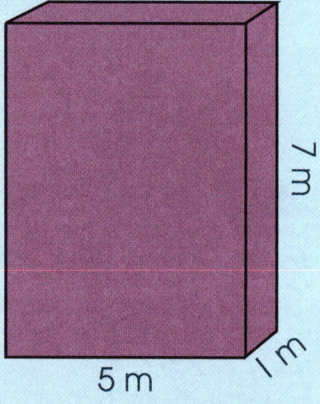
7 m
5 m
1 m

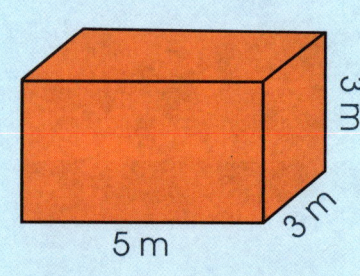
3 m
5 m
3 m

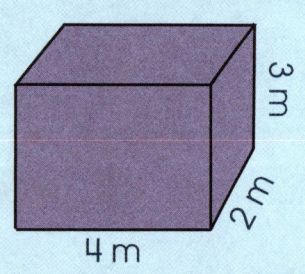
3 m
4 m
2 m

_____

_____

_____

Metric Measurement: Gram and Kilogram

Grams and **kilograms** are measurements of weight in the metric system. A gram (g) weighs about $\frac{1}{28}$ of an ounce. A grape or paper clip weighs about one gram. There are 1,000 grams in a kilogram. A kilogram (kg) weighs about 2.2 pounds. A brick weighs about 1 kilogram.

Directions: Choose grams or kilograms to measure the following.

Example:

grams

Metric Measurement: Milliliter and Liter

Liters and **milliliters** are measurements of liquid in the metric system. A milliliter (mL) equals 0.001 liter or 0.03 fluid ounces. A drop of water equals about 1 milliliter. Liters (L) measure large amounts of liquid. There are 1,000 milliliters in a liter. One liter measures 1.06 quarts. Soft drinks are often sold in 1-liter bottles.

Directions: Choose milliliters or liters to measure these liquids.

Example:

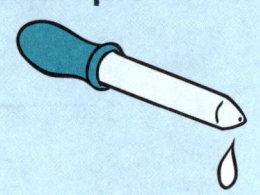 milliliters    _____

 _____    _____

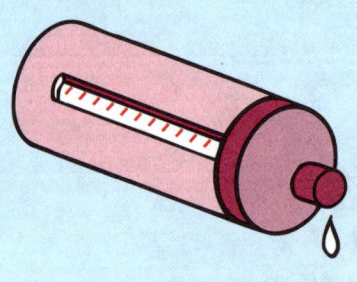 _____    _____

 _____    _____

Directions: Choose grams (g) or kilograms (kg) to weigh the following objects. The first one is done for you.

rhinoceros	**kg**	person	_____
dime	_____	airplane	_____
bucket of wet sand	_____	spider	_____
eyeglasses	_____	pair of scissors	_____
toy train engine	_____	horse	_____

Directions: Choose milliliters (mL) or liters (L) to measure the liquids in the following containers. The first one is done for you.

swimming pool	**L**	baby bottle	_____
small juice glass	_____	teapot	_____
gasoline tank	_____	outdoor fountain	_____
test tube	_____	ink pen	_____
washing machine	_____	Lake Erie	_____

Temperature: Celsius

Temperature measures how hot or cold something is. **Celsius** is used to measure temperature in the metric system. °C stands for degrees Celsius.

0°C

30°C

Directions: Use the thermometer to answer these questions.

At what temperature does water boil? _____

At what temperature does water freeze? _____

What is normal body temperature? _____

Is it a hot or cold day when the temperature is 42°C? _____

Is it a hot or cold day when the temperature is 5°C? _____

Which temperature best describes a hot summer day? 5°C 40°C 20°C _____

Which temperature best describes an icy winter day? 0°C 15°C 10°C _____

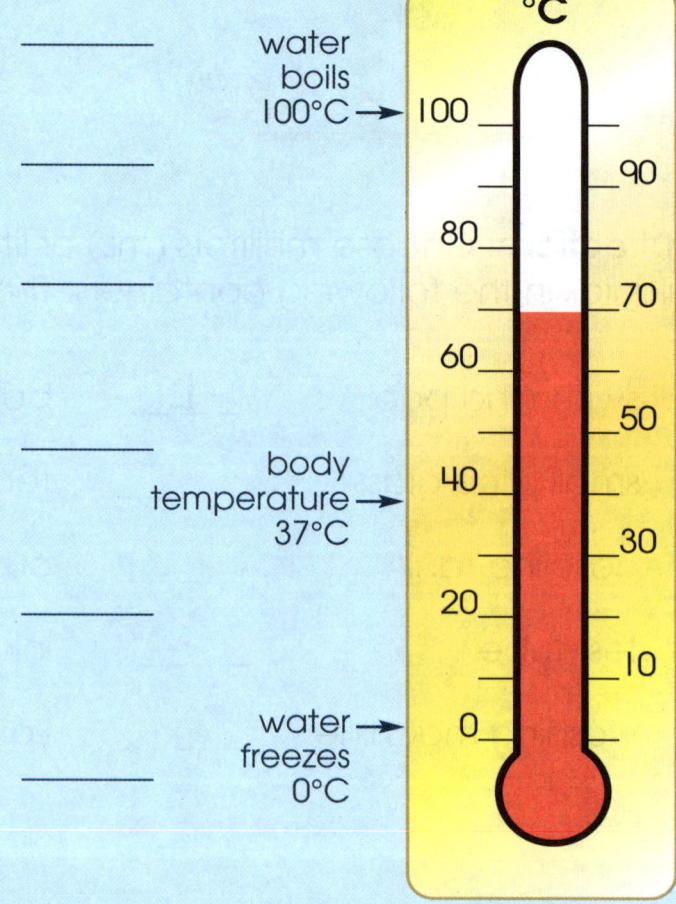

Fahrenheit is used to measure temperature in the standard system. °**F** stands for degrees Fahrenheit.

28°F

72°F

Directions: Use the thermometer to answer these questions.

At what temperature does water boil? _____

At what temperature does water freeze? _____

What is normal body temperature? _____

Is a 100°F day warm, hot, or cold? _____

Is a 0°F day warm, hot, or cold? _____

Which temperature best describes room temperature?
58°F 70°F 80°F _____

Which temperature best describes a cold winter day?
22°F 38°F 32°F _____

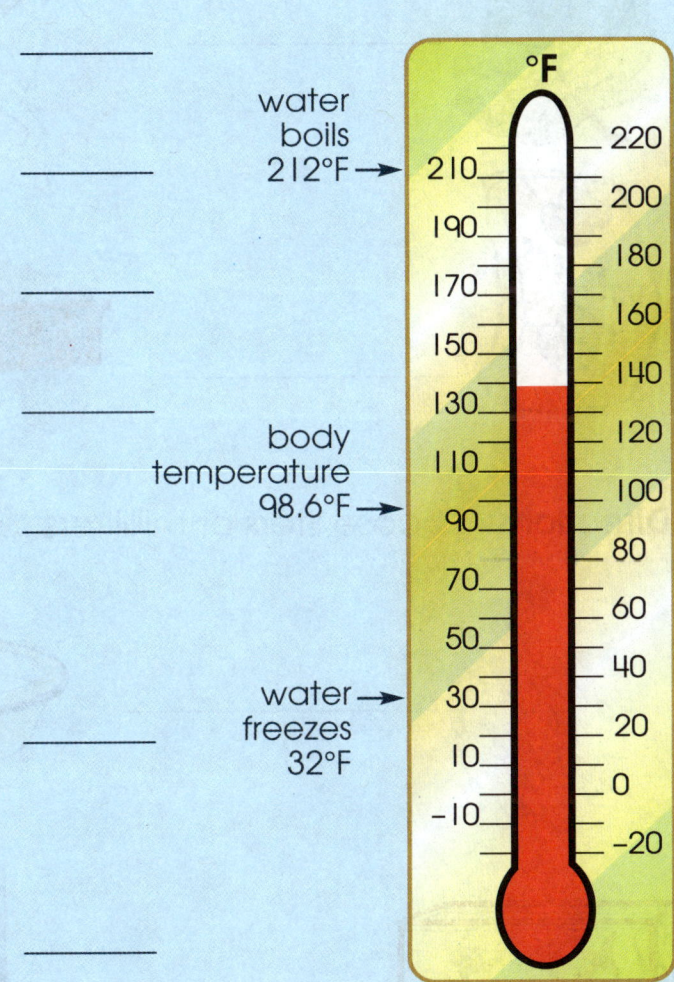

°F

water boils 212°F →

body temperature 98.6°F →

water → freezes 32°F

Review

Directions: Choose centimeters, meters, or kilometers to measure the following.

_____ height of a tree

_____ length of a shoe

_____ distance around Earth

_____ height of a building

_____ length of your yard

_____ distance a plane flies

Directions: Choose grams or kilograms to measure the following.

_____

_____

_____

_____

Directions: Choose liters or milliliters to measure the following.

_____

_____

_____

_____

A **graph** is a drawing that shows information about changes in numbers.

Directions: Answer the questions by reading the graphs.

Bar Graph

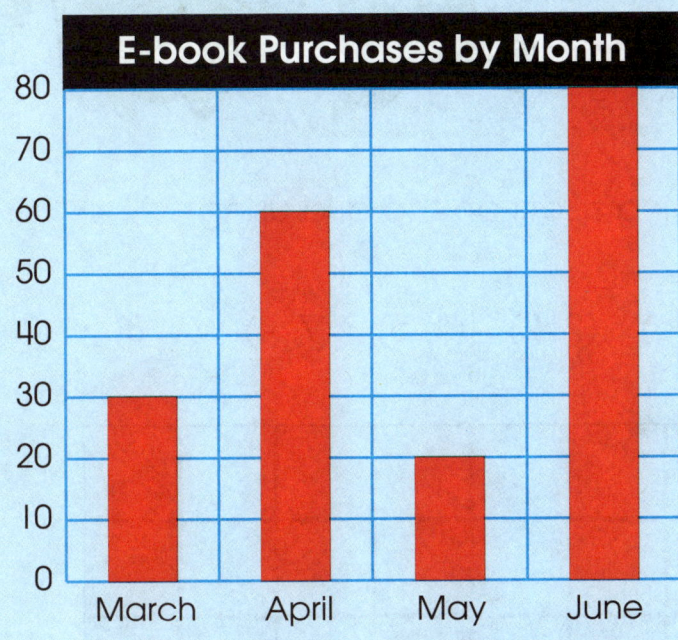

How many e-books were purchased in June?

_____

In which month were the fewest e-books purchased?

_____

How many e-books were sold for all 4 months?

_____

Line Graph

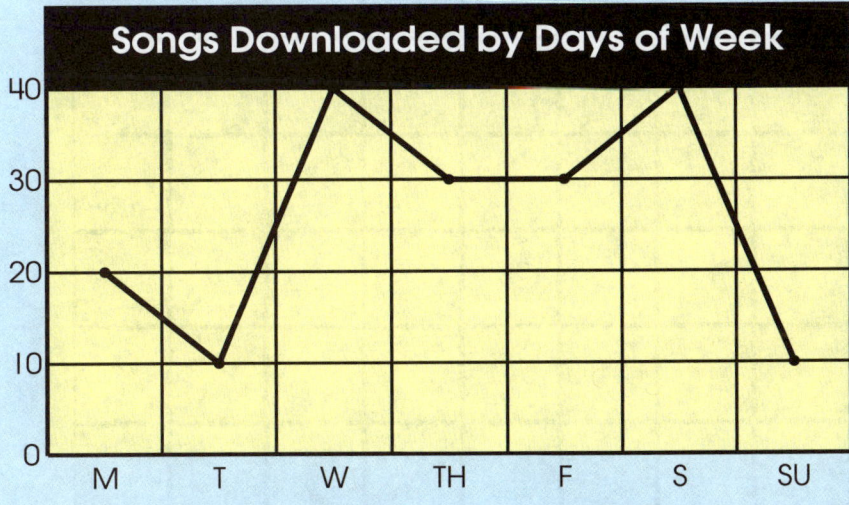

On which days were the fewest songs downloaded?

_____

How many songs were downloaded in 1 week?

_____

Ordered Pairs

An **ordered pair** is a pair of numbers used to locate a point.

Example: (8, 3)

Step 1: Count across to line 8 on the graph.
Step 2: Count up to line 3 on the graph.
Step 3: Draw a dot to mark the spot.

Directions: Map the following spots on the grid using ordered pairs.

(4, 7)   (9, 10)   (2, 1)   (5, 6)   (2, 2)   (1, 5)   (7, 4)   (3, 8)

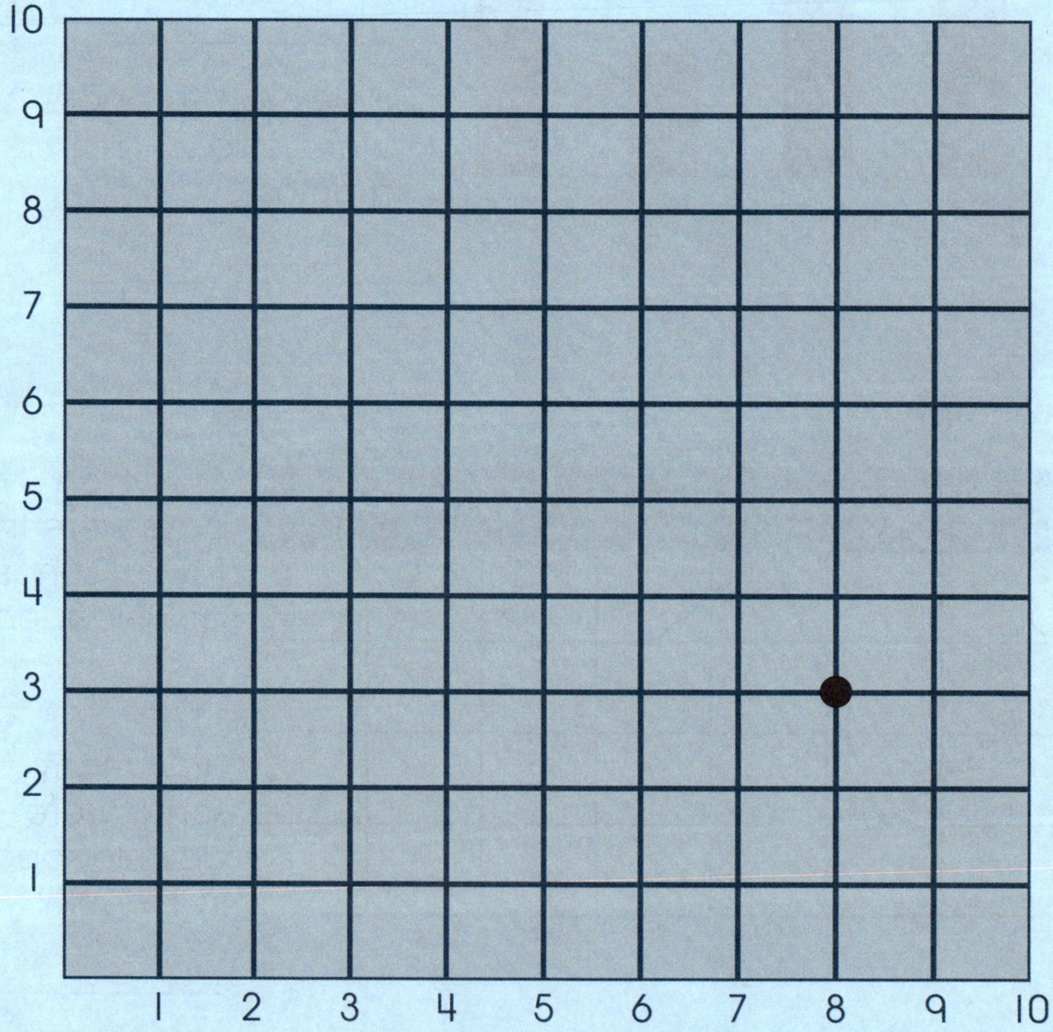

Graphs or grids are sometimes used to find the location of objects.

Example: The ice-cream cone is located at point (5, 6) on the graph. To find the ice cream's location, follow the line to the bottom of the grid to get the first number—5. Then, go back to the ice cream and follow the grid line to the left for the second number—6.

Directions: Write the ordered pair for the following objects. The first one is done for you.

book **(4, 8)**   bike _____   suitcase _____

house _____   globe _____   cup _____

Directions: Identify the objects located at the following points. The first one is done for you.

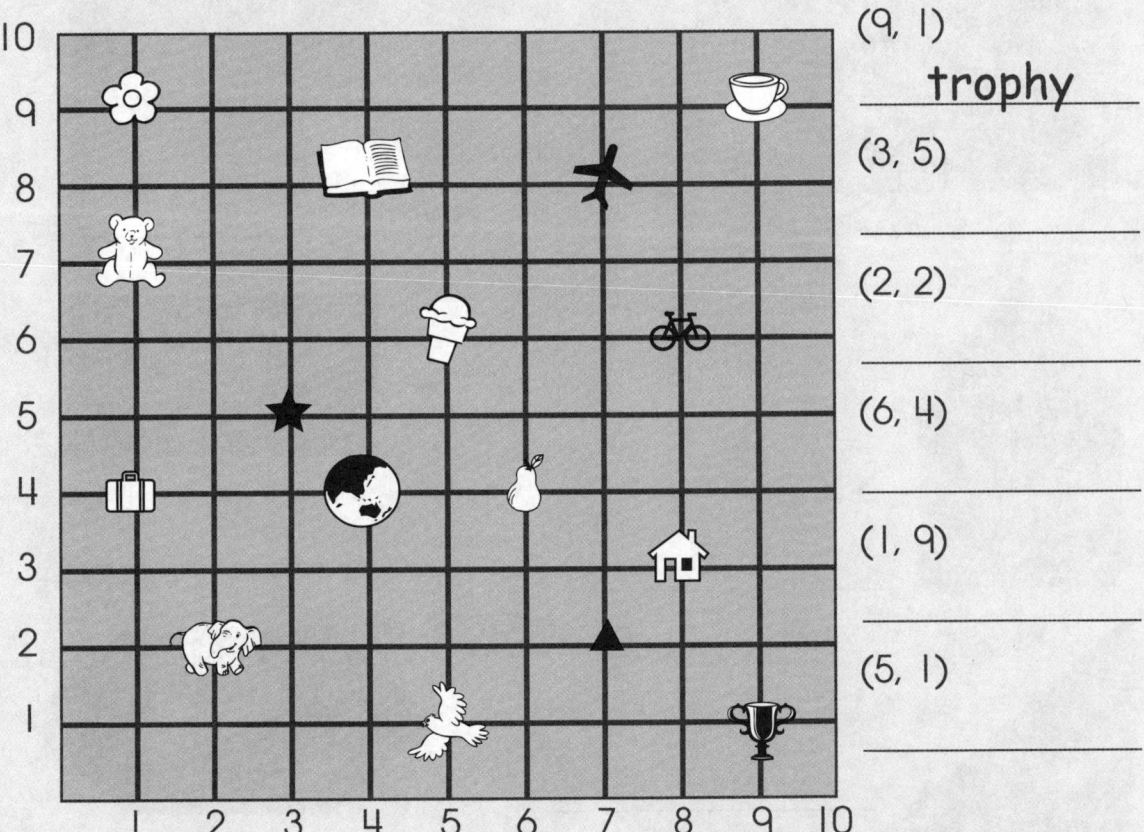

(9, 1)
____trophy____

(3, 5)
_____

(2, 2)
_____

(6, 4)
_____

(1, 9)
_____

(5, 1)
_____

Geometry: Polygons

A **polygon** is a closed figure with three or more sides.

Examples:

triangle
3 sides

square
4 equal sides

rectangle
4 sides

pentagon
5 sides

hexagon
6 sides

octagon
8 sides

Directions: Identify the polygons.

_____

_____

_____

_____

_____

A **line segment** has two end points.

A   B   Write: AB

A **line** has no end points and goes on in both directions.

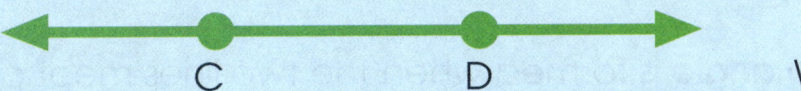

C   D   Write: CD

A **ray** is part of a line and goes on in one direction. It has one end point.

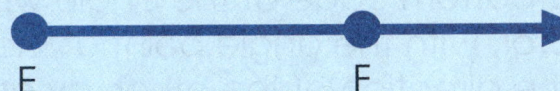

E   F   Write: EF

Directions: Identify each of the following as a line, line segment, or ray.

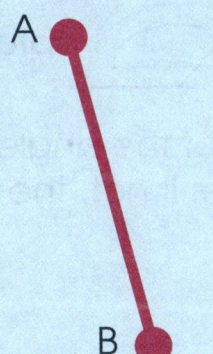

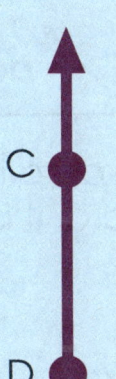

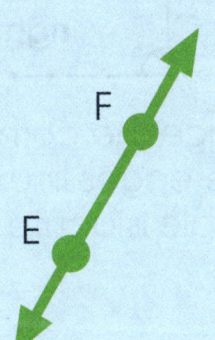

_____   _____   _____

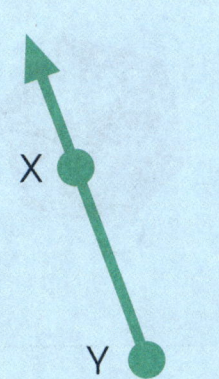

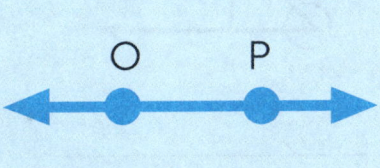

_____   _____   _____

Geometry: Angles

The point at which two line segments meet is called an **angle**. There are three types of angles—right, acute, and obtuse.

 A **right angle** is formed when the two lines meet at 90°.

 An **acute angle** is formed when the two lines meet at less than 90°.

 An **obtuse angle** is formed when the two lines meet at greater than 90°.

Angles can be measured with a protractor or index card. With a protractor, align the bottom edge of the angle with the bottom of the protractor, with the angle point at the circle of the protractor. Note the direction of the other ray and the number of degrees of the angle.

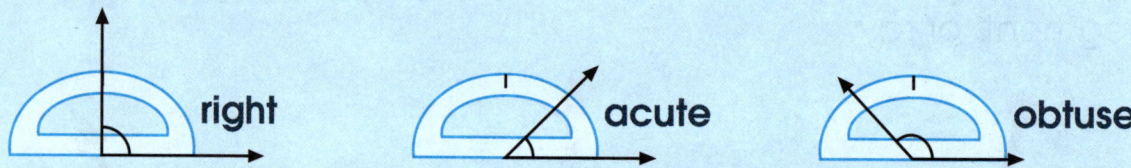

Place the corner of an index card in the corner of the angle. If the edges line up with the card, it is a right angle. If not, the angle is acute or obtuse.

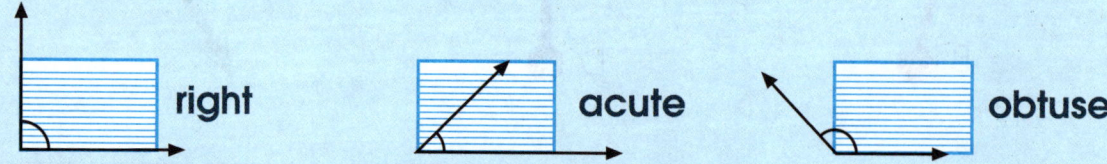

Directions: Use a protractor or index card to identify the following angles as right, obtuse, or acute.

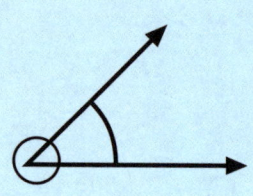  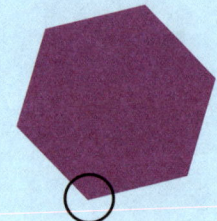

_____   _____   _____

Geometry: Circles

A **circle** is a round figure. It is named by its center. A **radius** is a line segment from the center of a circle to any point on the circle. A **diameter** is a line segment with both end points on the circle. The diameter always passes through the center of the circle.

Directions: Name the radius, diameter, and circle.

Example:

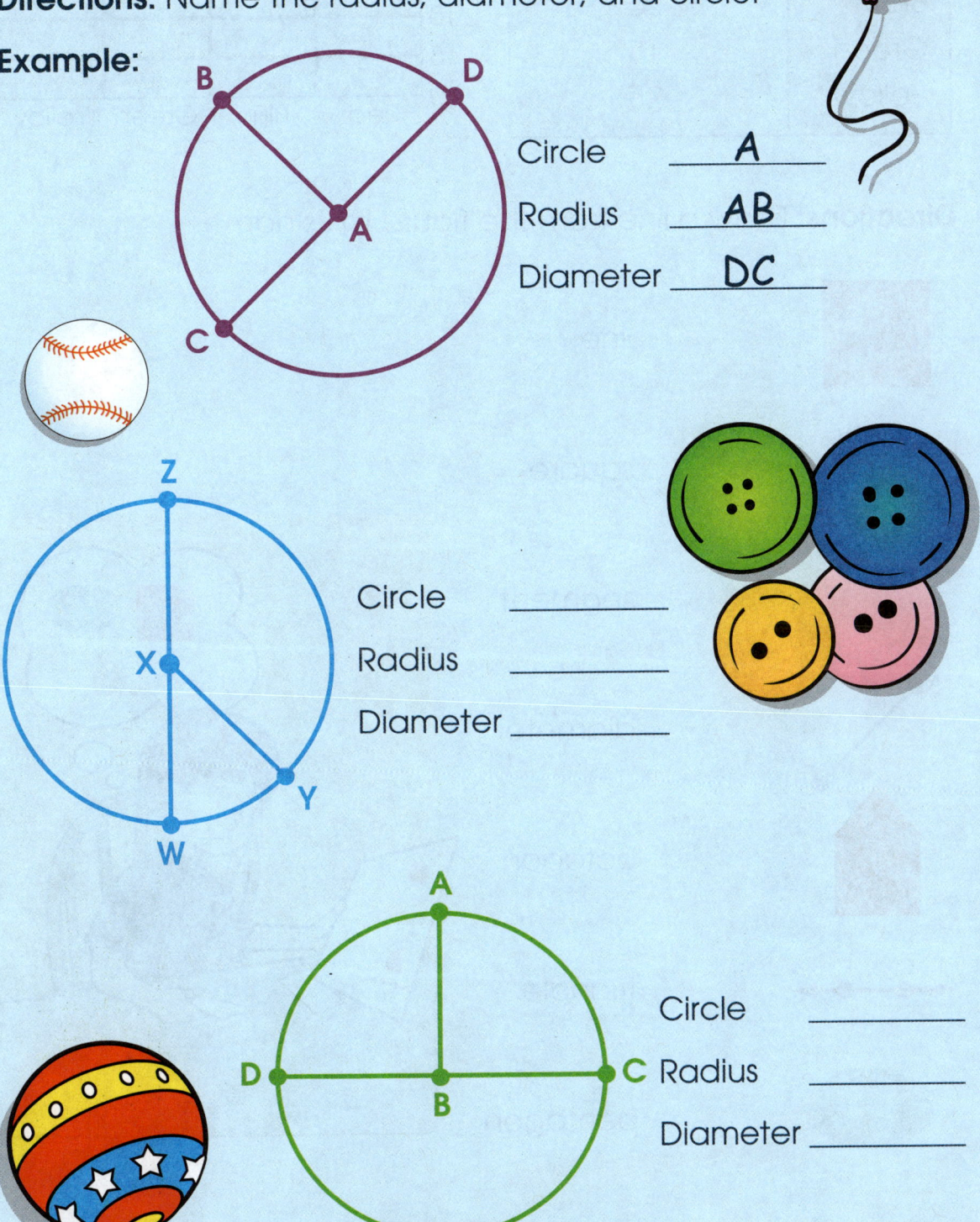

Circle ___A___

Radius ___AB___

Diameter ___DC___

Circle _____

Radius _____

Diameter _____

Circle _____

Radius _____

Diameter _____

Directions: Complete the graph using the information in the box.

Team	Games Played
Red	10
Blue	20
Green	15
Yellow	25

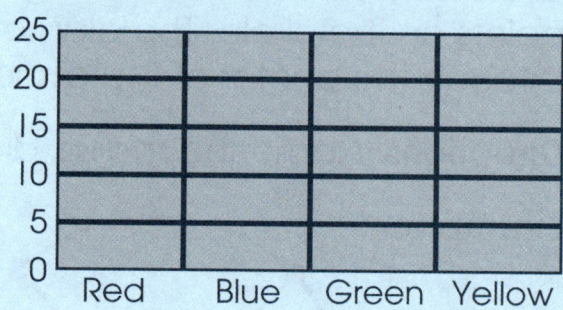

Directions: Draw a line from the figure to its name.

   line

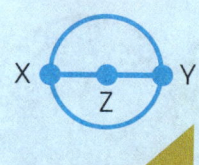   square

   segment

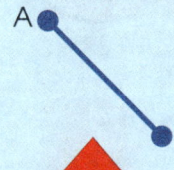   diameter

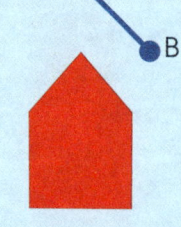   octagon

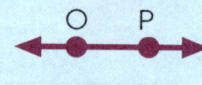   triangle

   pentagon

Acute Angle: An angle formed when two lines meet at less than 90°.

Addition: "Putting together" or adding two or more numbers to find the sum.

Angle: The point at which two line segments meet.

Area: The number of square units needed to cover a region.

Average: The result of adding two or more quantities and dividing by the number of quantities.

Celsius: A metric system measurement of temperature. °C stands for degrees Celsius.

Centimeter: A metric system measurement of length. There are 2.54 centimeters in an inch.

Circle: A round figure in which each point on the outside of the figure is an equal distance from the center of the figure.

Cup: A unit of volume in the standard system equal to 8 ounces.

Decimal: A number with one or more places to the right of a decimal point, such as 6.5 or 2.25.

Decimal Point: The dot between the ones place and the tenths place in a decimal.

Denominator: The number below the fraction bar in a fraction.

Diameter: A line segment that passes through the center of a circle and has both end points on the circle.

Difference: The answer in a subtraction problem.

Digits: The symbols used to write numbers: 0, 1, 2, 3, 4, 5, 6, 7, 8, 9.

Dividend: The larger number divided by the smaller number, or divisor, in a division problem. Example: 28 ÷ 7 = 4; 28 is the dividend.

Division: A way to find how many times one number is contained in another number.
For example, 28 ÷ 7 = 4 means that there are 4 groups of 7 in 28.

Equivalent Fractions: Two different fractions that represent the same number, such as $\frac{1}{2}$ and $\frac{2}{4}$.

Estimate: To give an approximate rather than an exact answer.

Factors: The numbers multiplied together in a multiplication problem.

Fahrenheit: A standard system measurement of temperature. °F stands for degrees Fahrenheit.

Foot (ft.): A unit of length in the standard system equal to 12 inches.

Fraction: A number that names part of a whole, such as $\frac{1}{2}$ or $\frac{1}{3}$.

Glossary

Gallon: A unit of liquid measure in the standard system equal to 4 quarts.

Gram (g): A metric system measurement of weight. One gram equals 0.001 kilogram or $\frac{1}{28}$ of an ounce.

Graph: A drawing that shows information about changes in numbers.

Hexagon: A polygon with six sides.

Inch (in.): A unit of length in the standard system equal to $\frac{1}{12}$ of a foot.

Kilogram (kg): A metric system measurement of weight. One kilogram equals 1,000 grams or 2.2 pounds.

Kilometer (km): A metric system measurement of length. One kilometer equals 1,000 meters or 0.62 mile.

Line: A line with no end points that goes on in both directions.

Line Segment: A line with two end points.

Liter (L): A metric system measurement of liquid. One liter equals 1,000 milliliters or 1.06 quarts.

Meter (m): A metric system measurement of length. One meter equals 39.37 inches.

Mile (mi.): A unit of length in the standard system equal to 1,760 yards or 5,280 feet.

Milliliter (mL): A metric system measurement of liquid. One milliliter equals 0.001 liter or 0.03 fluid ounce.

Mixed Number: A number written as a whole number and a fraction, such as $6\frac{5}{8}$.

Multiple: The product of a specific number and any other number. For example, the multiples of 2 are 2 (2 x 1), 4 (2 x 2), 6, 8, 10, 12, and so on.

Multiplication: A short way to find the sum of adding the same number a certain amount of times, such as 7 x 4 = 28 instead of 7 + 7 + 7 + 7 = 28.

Numerator: The number above the fraction bar in a fraction.

Obtuse Angle: An angle formed when two lines meet at greater than 90°.

Octagon: A polygon with eight sides.

Ordered Pair: A pair of numbers used to locate a point.

Ounce (oz.): A unit of measure in the standard system for weight. One ounce equals $\frac{1}{16}$ of a pound.

Pentagon: A polygon with five sides.

Glossary

Perimeter: The distance around a figure, found by adding the lengths of the sides.

Pint (pt.): A unit of liquid measure in the standard system equal to 2 cups.

Place Value: The value of a digit or numeral shown by where it is in a number.

Polygon: A closed figure with three or more sides.

Pound (lb.): A unit of measure in the standard system for weight. One pound equals 16 ounces.

Product: The answer in a multiplication problem.

Quart (qt.): A unit of liquid measure in the standard system equal to 4 cups or 2 pints.

Quotient: The answer in a division problem.

Radius: A line segment from the center of a circle to any point on the circle. It is equal to half the length of the diameter.

Ray: A part of a line that goes on in one direction. It has one end point.

Rectangle: A figure with four corners and four sides. The sides opposite one another are the same length.

Reduce: To divide by the greatest common factor in a fraction.

Regroup: To use 10 ones to form one 10, 10 tens to form one hundred, one 10 and 5 ones to form 15, and so on.

Remainder: The number left over in the quotient of a division problem.

Right Angle: An angle formed when two lines meet at 90°.

Rounding: Expressing a number to the nearest ten, hundred, thousand, and so on. For example, round 18 to 20; round 11 to 10.

Skip Counting: A quick way to count by skipping numbers.

Square: A figure with four corners and four sides of equal length.

Subtraction: "Taking away" or subtracting one number from another.

Sum: The answer in an addition problem.

Temperature: How hot or cold something is.

Ton: A unit of measure in the standard system for weight. One ton equals 2,000 pounds.

Triangle: A figure with three corners and three sides.

Volume: The number of cubic units that fit inside a figure.

Yard (yd.): A unit of distance in the standard system. There are 3 feet in a yard.

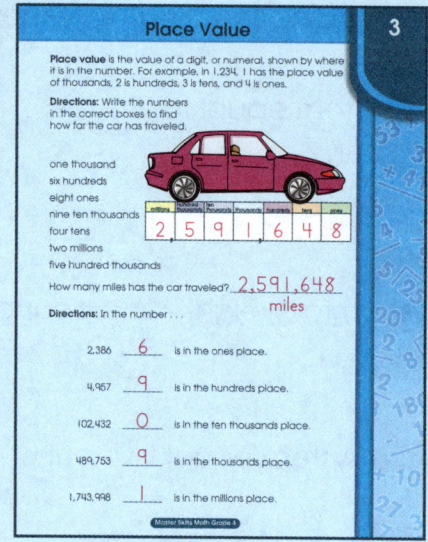

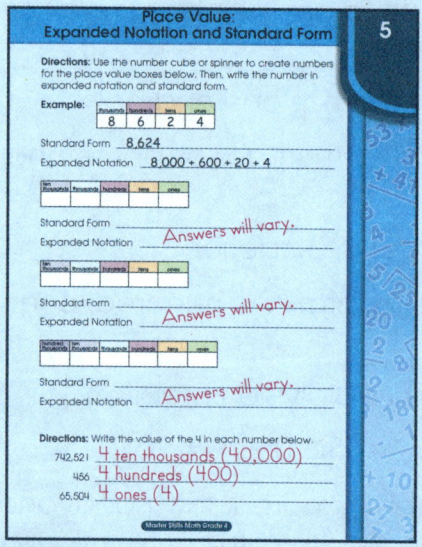

Answer Key

10 — Magic Squares

Directions: Some of the number squares below are "magic" and some are not. Squares that add up to the same number horizontally, vertically, and diagonally are "magic." Add the numbers horizontally and vertically in each square to discover which ones are "magic."

Example:

4	9	2	15
3	5	7	15
8	1	6	15
15	15	15	15

Magic? **yes**   1. Magic? **no**   2. Magic? **yes**

3. Magic? **yes**   4. Magic? **no**   5. Magic? **yes**

6. Magic? **yes**   7. Magic? **yes**   8. Magic? **no**

Challenge: Can you discover a pattern for number placement in the magic squares? Try to make a magic square of your own.

Master Skills Math Grade 4

---

11 — Adding Larger Numbers

When adding two-, three-, and four-digit numbers, add the ones first, then tens, hundreds, thousands, and so on.

Example:

Tens	Ones		Tens	Ones
5	4		5	4
+2	5		+2	5
	9		7	9

| 81 +23 | 67 +22 | 34 +82 | 730 +265 |
| 104 | 89 | 116 | 995 |

| 76 +73 | 1,803 +1,104 | 523 +476 | 267 +12 |
| 149 | 2,907 | 999 | 279 |

| 4,254 +545 | 111 +82 |
| 4,799 | 193 |

| 164 +425 | 727 +51 |
| 589 | 778 |

Master Skills Math Grade 4

12 — Addition: Regrouping

Regrouping uses 10 ones to form one 10, 10 tens to form one hundred, one 10 and 5 ones to form 15, and so on.

Directions: Add using regrouping. Color in all the boxes with a 5 in the answer to help the dog find its way home.

| 63 +22 | 5,268 4,410 +1,683 | 248 +463 | 291 +543 |
| 85 | 11,861 | 711 | 834 |

| 1,736 +5,367 | 2,946 +7,384 | 3,245 1,239 +981 | 738 +692 | 896 +728 |
| 7,103 | 10,330 | 5,465 | 1,430 | 1,624 |

| 2,603 +5,004 | 4,507 +289 | 1,483 +6,753 | 1,258 +6,301 | 464 +6,002 |
| 7,607 | 4,796 | 8,236 | 7,559 | 6,498 |

| 782 +65 | 485 +276 | 3,421 +8,064 |
| 847 | 761 | 11,485 |

| 48 93 +26 | 90 263 +864 | 362 453 +800 |
| 167 | 1,217 | 1,615 |

Master Skills Math Grade 4

13 — Subtraction

Subtraction is "taking away" or subtracting one number from another.

Directions: Complete the following problems as quickly as you can.

| 18 −9 | 13 −6 | 12 −5 | 17 −8 | 16 −8 |
| 9 | 7 | 7 | 9 | 8 |

| 12 −5 | 10 −4 | 5 −3 | 14 −6 | 15 −9 |
| 7 | 6 | 2 | 8 | 6 |

| 9 −5 | 8 −3 | 6 −2 | 9 −4 | 10 −7 |
| 4 | 5 | 4 | 5 | 3 |

| 11 −4 | 12 −8 | 16 −9 | 11 −8 | 10 −10 |
| 7 | 4 | 7 | 3 | 0 |

How quickly did you complete this page? _____

Master Skills Math Grade 4

14 — Subtracting Larger Numbers

When you subtract larger numbers, subtract the ones first, then the tens, hundreds, thousands, and so on.

Example:

Tens	Ones		Tens	Ones
9	4		9	4
−2	1		−2	1
	3		7	3

Directions: Solve these subtraction problems.

| 29 −26 | 99 −58 | 359 −55 |
| 3 | 41 | 304 |

| 735 −734 | 849 −726 | 7,678 −4,321 |
| 1 | 123 | 3,557 |

| 865 −731 | 55 −25 | 9,876 −1,234 |
| 134 | 30 | 8,642 |

Master Skills Math Grade 4

---

15 — Subtraction: Regrouping

Directions: Subtract using regrouping.

Examples:

| 23 −18 | 2̶3̸ −18 | 243 −96 | 2̶4̸3̸ −96 |
| | 5 | | 5 |

| 76 −49 | 94 −38 | 156 −77 | 341 −83 | 726 −29 |
| 27 | 56 | 79 | 258 | 697 |

| 806 −738 | 743 −550 | 903 −336 | 647 −289 | 254 −69 |
| 68 | 193 | 567 | 358 | 185 |

| 961 −846 | 573 −76 | 604 −55 | 265 −19 | 372 −59 |
| 115 | 497 | 549 | 246 | 313 |

| 358 −99 | 147 −49 |
| 259 | 98 |

Master Skills Math Grade 4

Master Skills Math Grade 4

Answer Key

16 — Addition and Subtraction

Directions: Add or subtract, using regrouping when needed.

32 + 68 + 43 = **143**	183 + 246 + 89 = **518**	456 + 398 + 597 = **1,451**
643 − 377 = **266**	1,563 − 941 = **622**	3,586 + 4,218 = **7,804**
8,711 − 4,937 = **3,774**	9,361 − 7,452 = **1,909**	5,734 + 6,298 = **12,032**
293 + 431 + 93 = **817**	743 − 529 = **214**	849 + 250 + 82 = **1,181**

68 + 93 + 146 = **307**

43 + 745 − 29 = **759**

156 + 627 + 541 = **1,324**

Tom walks 389 steps from his house to the store. It is 149 steps to Elm Street. It is 52 steps from Maple Street to the store. How many steps is it from Elm Street to Maple Street? **188 steps**

17 — Addition and Subtraction

Directions: Add or subtract, using regrouping when needed.

38 + 43 + 21 = **102**	1,269 + 2,453 + 8,219 = **11,941**	5,792 − 4,814 = **978**	629 + 491 + 308 = **1,428**	4,697 − 2,988 = **1,709**
5,280 − 3,147 = **2,133**	68 + 27 + 42 = **137**	197 + 436 + 213 = **846**	7,321 − 2,789 = **4,532**	456 + 974 = **1,430**
3,932 + 4,681 = **8,613**	863 + 492 + 57 = **1,412**	9,873 + 5,483 = **15,356**	4,978 + 2,131 = **7,109**	6,235 + 2,986 = **9,221**

Sue stocked her pond with 263 bass and 187 trout. The turtles ate 97 fish. How many fish are left? **353 fish**

18 — Rounding: Tens

Rounding a number means expressing it to the nearest ten, hundred, thousand, and so on. Rounding makes estimating sums, differences, and products easier. When rounding to the nearest ten, the key number is in the ones place. If the ones digit is 5 or larger, round up to the nearest ten. If the ones digit is 4 or less, round down to the nearest ten.

Example:
Round 81 to the nearest ten.
• 1 is the key digit.
• If it is less than 5, round down.
• Answer: 80

Directions: Round these numbers to the nearest ten.

41 → **40**, 32 → **30**, 75 → **80**, 481 → **480**, 165 → **170**, 29 → **30**, 89 → **90**, 17 → **20**, 38 → **40**, 68 → **70**, 52 → **50**, 573 → **570**, 98 → **100**, 87 → **90**, 43 → **40**, 12 → **10**

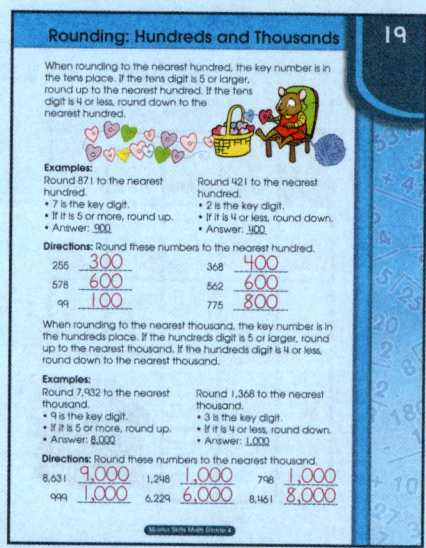

19 — Rounding: Hundreds and Thousands

When rounding to the nearest hundred, the key number is in the tens place. If the tens digit is 5 or larger, round up to the nearest hundred. If the tens digit is 4 or less, round down to the nearest hundred.

Examples:
Round 871 to the nearest hundred.
• 7 is the key digit.
• If it is 5 or more, round up.
• Answer: 900

Round 421 to the nearest hundred.
• 2 is the key digit.
• If it is 4 or less, round down.
• Answer: 400

Directions: Round these numbers to the nearest hundred.

255 → **300**, 368 → **400**, 578 → **600**, 562 → **600**, 99 → **100**, 775 → **800**

When rounding to the nearest thousand, the key number is in the hundreds place. If the hundreds digit is 5 or larger, round up to the nearest thousand. If the hundreds digit is 4 or less, round down to the nearest thousand.

Examples:
Round 7,932 to the nearest thousand.
• 9 is the key digit.
• If it is 5 or more, round up.
• Answer: 8,000

Round 1,368 to the nearest thousand.
• 3 is the key digit.
• If it is 4 or less, round down.
• Answer: 1,000

Directions: Round these numbers to the nearest thousand.

8,631 → **9,000**, 1,248 → **1,000**, 798 → **1,000**, 999 → **1,000**, 6,229 → **6,000**, 8,161 → **8,000**

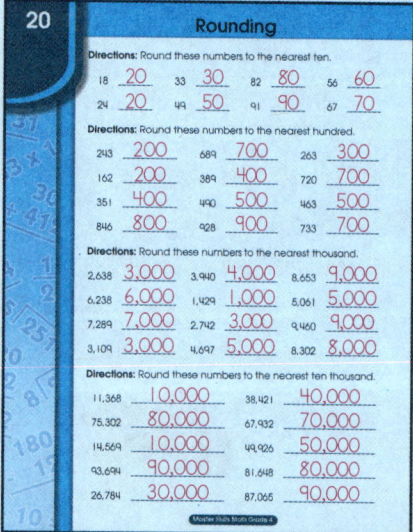

20 — Rounding

Directions: Round these numbers to the nearest ten.

18 → **20**, 33 → **30**, 82 → **80**, 56 → **60**, 24 → **20**, 43 → **50**, 91 → **90**, 67 → **70**

Directions: Round these numbers to the nearest hundred.

243 → **200**, 689 → **700**, 263 → **300**, 162 → **200**, 389 → **400**, 720 → **700**, 351 → **400**, 460 → **500**, 463 → **500**, 846 → **800**, 928 → **900**, 733 → **700**

Directions: Round these numbers to the nearest thousand.

2,638 → **3,000**, 3,940 → **4,000**, 8,653 → **9,000**, 6,238 → **6,000**, 1,429 → **1,000**, 5,061 → **5,000**, 7,289 → **7,000**, 2,742 → **3,000**, 9,460 → **9,000**, 3,109 → **3,000**, 4,697 → **5,000**, 8,302 → **8,000**

Directions: Round these numbers to the nearest ten thousand.

11,368 → **10,000**, 38,421 → **40,000**, 75,302 → **80,000**, 67,932 → **70,000**, 14,569 → **10,000**, 49,926 → **50,000**, 93,694 → **90,000**, 81,648 → **80,000**, 26,784 → **30,000**, 87,065 → **90,000**

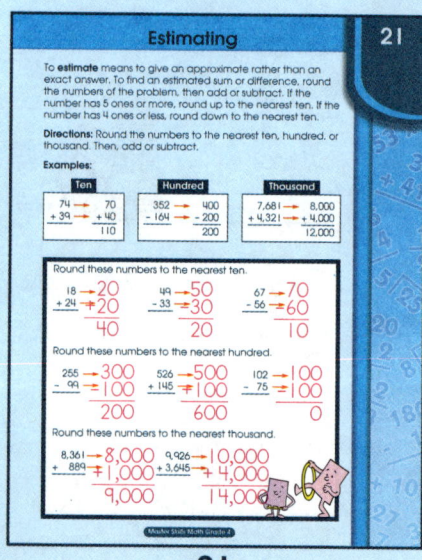

21 — Estimating

To estimate means to give an approximate rather than an exact answer. To find an estimated sum or difference, round the numbers of the problem, then add or subtract. If the number has 5 ones or more, round up to the nearest ten. If the number has 4 ones or less, round down to the nearest ten.

Directions: Round the numbers to the nearest ten, hundred, or thousand. Then, add or subtract.

Examples:

Ten	Hundred	Thousand
74 → 70, + 39 → 40 = 110	352 → 400, − 164 → 200 = 200	7,681 → 8,000, + 4,321 → 4,000 = 12,000

Round these numbers to the nearest ten.

18 → 20, + 24 → 20 = **40**; 49 → 50, − 33 → 30 = **20**; 67 → 70, − 56 → 60 = **10**

Round these numbers to the nearest hundred.

255 → 300, − 99 → 100 = **200**; 526 → 500, + 145 → 100 = **600**; 102 → 100, − 75 → 100 = **0**

Round these numbers to the nearest thousand.

8,361 → 8,000, + 889 → 1,000 = **9,000**; 9,645 → 10,000, + 3,645 → 4,000 = **14,000**

Answer Key

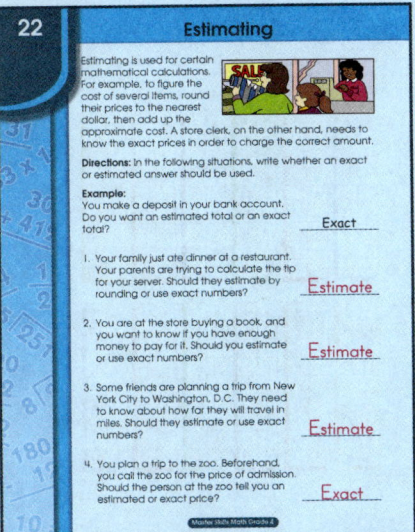

22

23

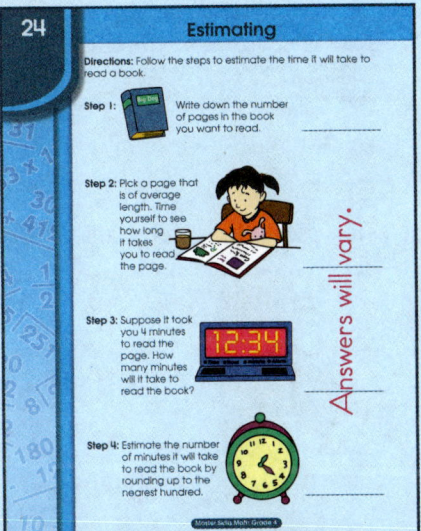

24

Skip Counting

25

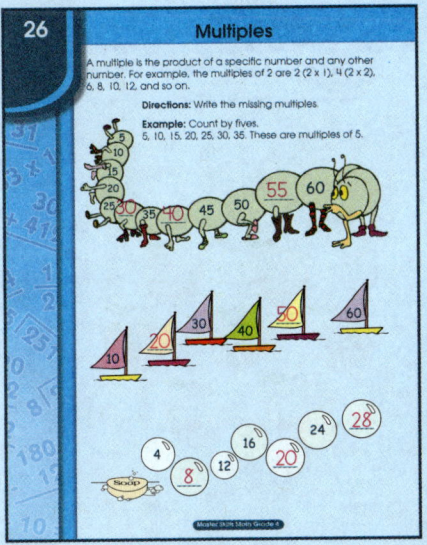

26

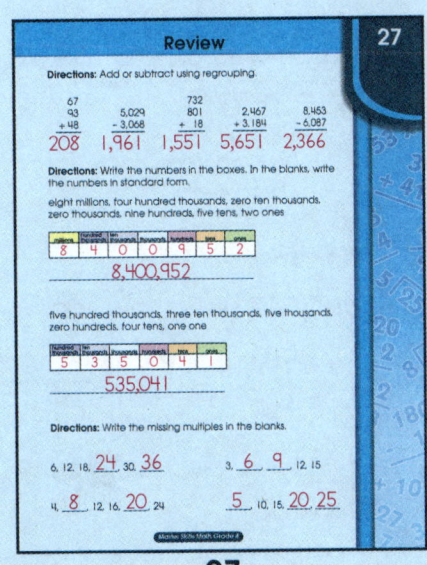

27

28 — Multiplication

Multiplication is a short way to find the sum of adding the same number a certain amount of times, such as 7 × 4 = 28 instead of 7 + 7 + 7 + 7 = 28.

Directions: Multiply as quickly as you can.

4 ×7 = 28	7 ×6 = 42	0 ×8 = 0	9 ×2 = 14	5 ×9 = 45	1 ×5 = 5
8 ×3 = 24	7 ×1 = 7	4 ×2 = 8	9 ×6 = 54	8 ×5 = 40	6 ×7 = 42
3 ×5 = 15	7 ×8 = 56	3 ×9 = 27	5 ×6 = 30	9 ×9 = 81	7 ×5 = 35

3 ×6 = 18   2 ×8 = 16   8 ×6 = 48

0 ×7 = 0   3 ×3 = 9

How quickly did you complete this page? Answers will vary.

Master Skills Math Grade 4

28

29 — Fact Factory

Factors are the numbers multiplied together in a multiplication problem. The product is the answer.

Directions: Write the missing factors or products.

Master Skills Math Grade 4

29

30 — Multiplication: Tens, Hundreds, Thousands

When multiplying a number by 10, the answer is the number with a 0. It is like counting by tens.

Examples:

| 10 ×1 = 10 | 10 ×2 = 20 | 10 ×3 = 30 | 10 ×4 = 40 | 10 ×5 = 50 | 10 ×6 = 60 |

When multiplying a number by 100, the answer is the number with two 0's. When multiplying by 1,000, the answer is the number with three 0's.

Examples:

| 100 ×1 = 100 | 100 ×2 = 200 | 100 ×3 = 300 | 1,000 ×1 = 1,000 | 1,000 ×2 = 2,000 | 1,000 ×3 = 3,000 |

Directions: Multiply.

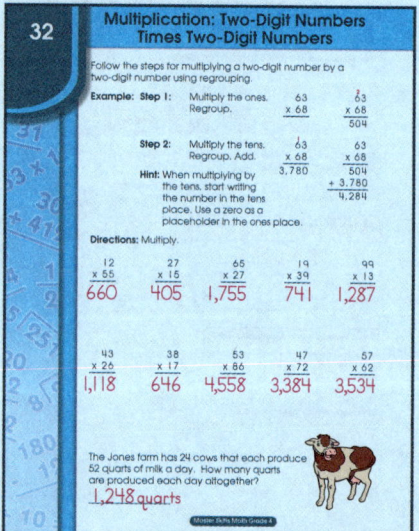

10 ×3 = 30   60 ×5 = 300   700 ×8 = 5,600
400 ×5 = 2,000
80 ×9 = 720   4,000 ×2 = 8,000   6,000 ×4 = 24,000   50 ×7 = 350
300 ×9 = 2,700   700 ×6 = 4,200

Master Skills Math Grade 4

30

31 — Multiplication: One-Digit Numbers Times Two-Digit Numbers

Follow the steps for multiplying a one-digit number by a two-digit number using regrouping.

Example: Step 1: Multiply the ones. Regroup.   54 ×7 = 8

Step 2: Multiply the tens. Add two tens.   54 ×7 = 378

Directions: Multiply.

| 27 ×3 = 81 | 63 ×4 = 252 | 52 ×5 = 260 | 91 ×9 = 819 | 45 ×7 = 315 |
| 64 ×5 = 320 | 76 ×3 = 228 | 93 ×6 = 558 | 87 ×4 = 348 | 66 ×7 = 462 |

47 ×8 = 376   64 ×9 = 576   51 ×8 = 408

13 ×7 = 91   32 ×4 = 128   25 ×8 = 200

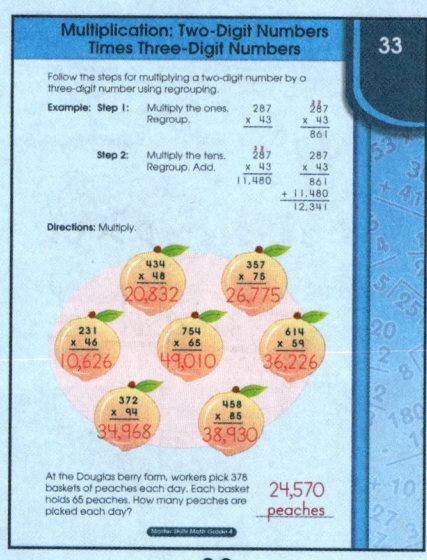

The chickens on the Smith farm produce 48 dozen eggs each day. How many dozen eggs do they produce in 7 days?   336 eggs

Master Skills Math Grade 4

31

32 — Multiplication: Two-Digit Numbers Times Two-Digit Numbers

Follow the steps for multiplying a two-digit number by a two-digit number using regrouping.

Example: Step 1: Multiply the ones. Regroup.   63 ×68 = 504

Step 2: Multiply the tens. Regroup. Add.   63 ×68 = 504 + 3,780 = 4,284

Hint: When multiplying by the tens, start writing the number in the tens place. Use a zero as a placeholder in the ones place.

Directions: Multiply.

| 12 ×55 = 660 | 27 ×15 = 405 | 65 ×27 = 1,755 | 19 ×39 = 741 | 99 ×13 = 1,287 |
| 43 ×26 = 1,118 | 38 ×17 = 646 | 53 ×86 = 4,558 | 47 ×72 = 3,384 | 57 ×62 = 3,534 |

The Jones farm has 24 cows that each produce 52 quarts of milk a day. How many quarts are produced each day altogether?   1,248 quarts

Master Skills Math Grade 4

32

33 — Multiplication: Two-Digit Numbers Times Three-Digit Numbers

Follow the steps for multiplying a two-digit number by a three-digit number using regrouping.

Example: Step 1: Multiply the ones. Regroup.   287 ×43 = 861

Step 2: Multiply the tens. Regroup. Add.   287 ×43 = 861 + 11,480 = 12,341

Directions: Multiply.

434 ×48 = 20,832   357 ×75 = 26,775
231 ×46 = 10,626   754 ×65 = 49,010   614 ×59 = 36,226
372 ×94 = 34,968   458 ×85 = 38,930

At the Douglas berry farm, workers pick 378 baskets of peaches each day. Each basket holds 65 peaches. How many peaches are picked each day?   24,570 peaches

Master Skills Math Grade 4

33

34 — Multiplication: Two-Digit Numbers Times Two- and Three-Digit Numbers

Directions: Multiply.

25 × 72 = **1,800**	70 × 66 = **4,620**	844 × 24 = **20,256**	124 × 15 = **1,860**
45 × 41 = **1,845**	76 × 78 = **5,928**	74 × 69 = **5,106**	
261 × 88 = **22,968**	48 × 36 = **1,728**	263 × 57 = **14,991**	
37 × 64 = **2,368**	52 × 43 = **2,236**	321 × 78 = **25,038**	
544 × 58 = **31,552**	797 × 24 = **19,128**	998 × 37 = **36,926**	

34

35 — Multiplication: Two-Digit Numbers Times Three-Digit Numbers

Directions: Multiply. Regroup when needed.

Example:
```
    563
  × 248
  4,504
 22,520
+112,600
139,624
```

Hint: When multiplying by the tens, start writing the number in the tens place. When multiplying by the hundreds, start in the hundreds place.

| 842 × 167 = **140,614** | 932 × 272 = **253,504** | 759 × 468 = **355,212** | 531 × 556 = **295,236** |
| 383 × 476 = **182,308** | 523 × 349 = **182,527** | 229 × 189 = **43,281** | 738 × 513 = **378,594** |

James grows pumpkins on his farm. He has 362 rows of pumpkins. There are 593 pumpkins in each row. How many pumpkins does James grow?   **214,666 pumpkins**

35

36 — Multiplication Practice

Directions: Multiply. Use the code to color the quilt.

70,725 — **red**   667 — **green**   448 — **white**
249,738 — **orange**   34,088 — **blue**   221,446 — **yellow**

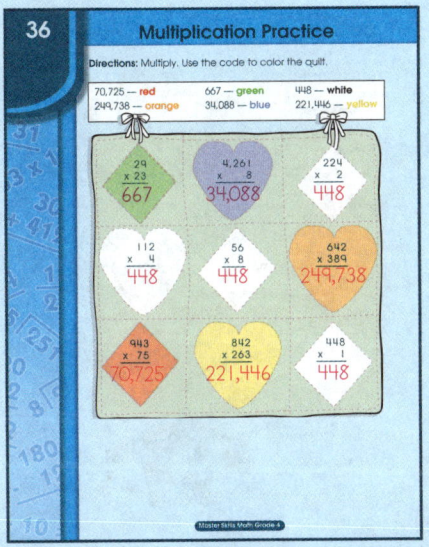

29 × 23 = **667**	4,261 × 8 = **34,088**	224 × 2 = **448**
112 × 4 = **448**	56 × 8 = **448**	642 × 389 = **249,738**
943 × 75 = **70,725**	842 × 263 = **221,446**	448 × 1 = **448**

36

37 — Multiplication Drill

Directions: Multiply.

134 × 22 = **2,948**	48 × 66 = **3,168**	876 × 13 = **11,388**	432 × 64 = **27,648**
68 × 11 = **748**	5,478 × 8 = **43,824**	248 × 61 = **15,128**	6,897 × 6 = **41,382**
82 × 4 = **328**	6,798 × 5 = **33,990**	79 × 86 = **6,794**	694 × 38 = **26,372**

Directions: Color the picture by matching each number with its paintbrush.

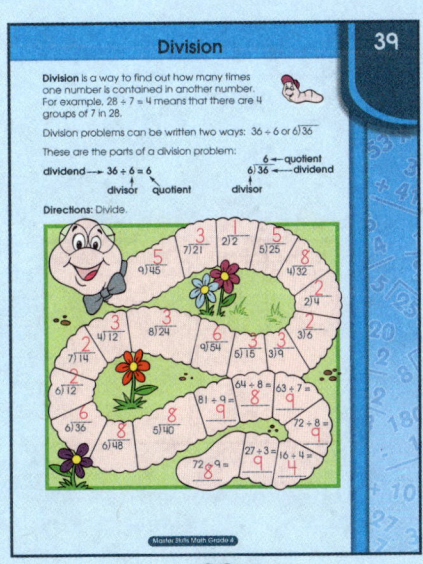

37

38 — Review

Directions: Multiply. Use the box to solve the problem. Color the ribbons blue if the answer is correct.

5,683 × 9 = **51,147**	5,683 × 9 = **51,147**	256 × 38 = **8,728**	256 × 38 = **9,728**
356 × 427 = **152,012**	356 × 427 = **152,012**	800 × 7 = **6,300**	800 × 7 = **5,600**
489 × 56 = **27,384**	489 × 56 = **27,384**	60 × 5 = **300**	60 × 5 = **300**

38

39 — Division

Division is a way to find out how many times one number is contained in another number. For example, 28 ÷ 7 = 4 means that there are 4 groups of 7 in 28.

Division problems can be written two ways: 36 ÷ 6 or 6⟌36

These are the parts of a division problem:

dividend → 36 ÷ 6 = 6 ← quotient, divisor

6 ← quotient, 6⟌36 ← dividend, divisor

Directions: Divide.

39

Answer Key

40

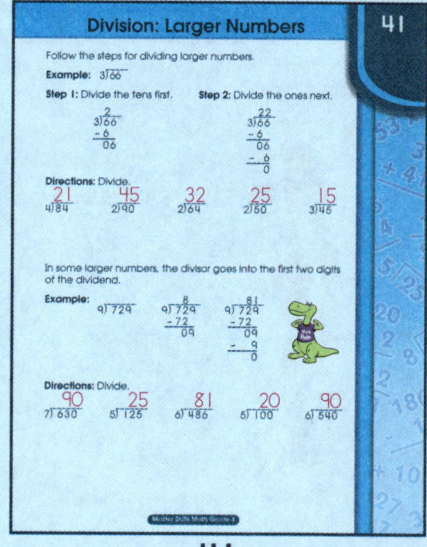

41

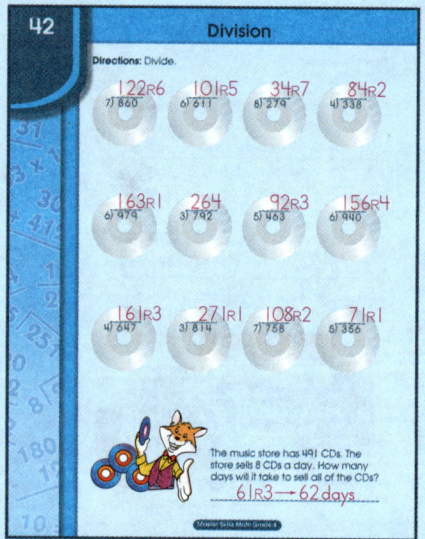

42

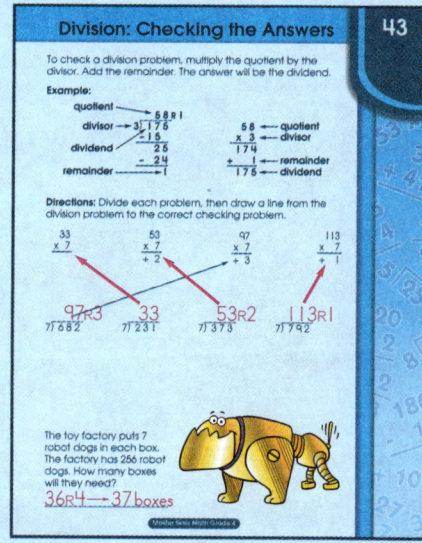

43

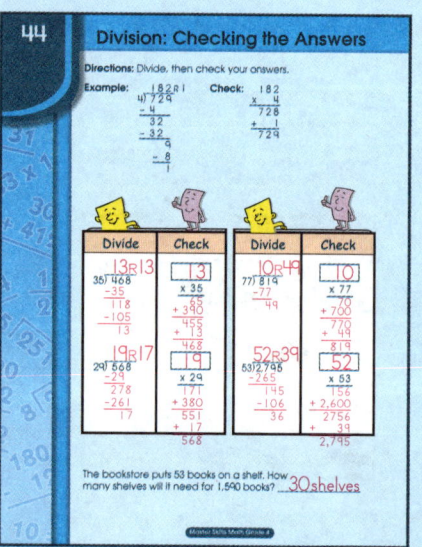

44

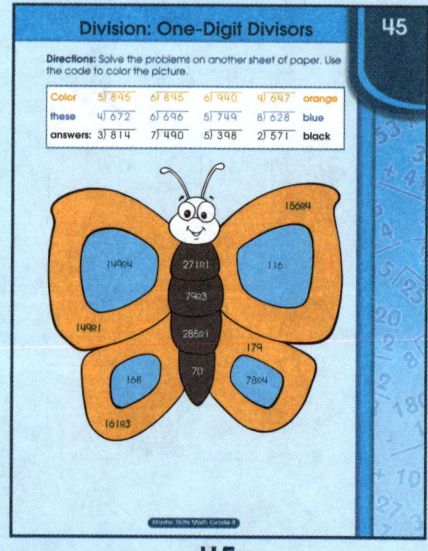

45

46 — Division: Two-Digit Divisors

Directions: Divide. Then, check each answer on another sheet of paper by multiplying it by the divisor and adding the remainder.

The Allen farm has 882 chickens. The chickens are kept in 21 coops. How many chickens are there in each coop? **42 chickens**

46

47 — Averaging

An **average** is found by adding two or more quantities and dividing by the number of quantities.

Example:
Step 1: Find the sum of the numbers. 24 + 36 + 30 = 90
Step 2: Divide by the number of quantities. 90 ÷ 3 = 30
The average is 30.

Directions: Find the average of each group of numbers. Draw a line from each problem to the correct average.

A baseball player had 3 hits in game one, 2 hits in game two, and 4 hits in game three. How many hits did she average over the three games? **3 hits**

47

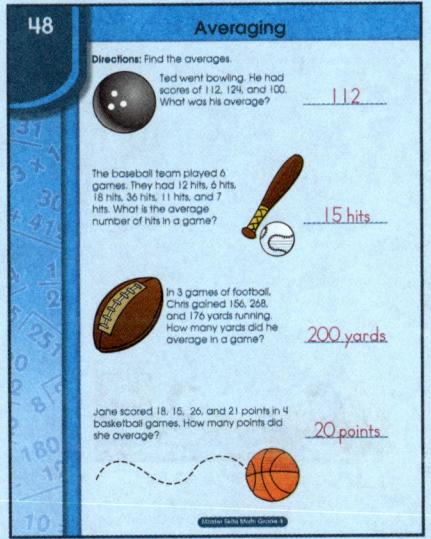

48 — Averaging

Directions: Find the averages.

Ted went bowling. He had scores of 112, 124, and 100. What was his average? **112**

The baseball team played 6 games. They had 12 hits, 6 hits, 18 hits, 36 hits, 11 hits, and 7 hits. What is the average number of hits in a game? **15 hits**

In 3 games of football, Chris gained 156, 268, and 176 yards running. How many yards did he average in a game? **200 yards**

Jane scored 18, 15, 26, and 21 points in 4 basketball games. How many points did she average? **20 points**

48

50 — Review

Directions: Divide.

Directions: Find the averages.

22, 38 **30**   105, 263, 331 **233**
248, 325, 250, 69 **223**   17, 18, 36, 28, 6 **21**

50

52 — Fractions

Directions: Name the fraction that is shaded.

Examples:
3 of 4 equal parts are shaded.
12 of 16 equal parts are shaded.

52

57 — Fractions: Addition

When adding fractions with the same denominator, the denominator stays the same. Add only the numerators.

Example: numerator / denominator   1/3 + 2/3 = 3/3

Directions: Add the fractions on the flowers. Begin in the center of each flower and add each petal. The first one is done for you.

57

Answer Key

58 — Fractions: Subtraction

When subtracting fractions with the same denominator, the denominator stays the same. Subtract only the numerators.

Directions: Solve the problems, working from left to right. As you find each answer, copy the letter from the key into the numbered blanks. The answer is the name of a famous American. The first one is done for you.

T $\frac{1}{8}$	P $\frac{5}{24}$	H $\frac{1}{4}$	F $\frac{4}{12}$	E $\frac{7}{9}$
J $\frac{3}{12}$	E $\frac{3}{9}$	O $\frac{2}{9}$	F $\frac{8}{4}$	R $\frac{7}{16}$
O $\frac{2}{8}$	Y $\frac{8}{20}$	Q $\frac{1}{32}$	M $\frac{1}{3}$	S $\frac{5}{20}$
A $\frac{4}{12}$	R $\frac{12}{16}$	S $\frac{3}{6}$	N $\frac{2}{6}$	O $\frac{11}{15}$

1. $\frac{3}{8} - \frac{2}{8} = \frac{1}{8}$ 6. $\frac{6}{9} - \frac{1}{9} = \frac{5}{9}$ 11. $\frac{4}{7} - \frac{2}{7} = \frac{2}{7}$

2. $\frac{2}{4} - \frac{1}{4} = \frac{1}{4}$ 7. $\frac{6}{12} - \frac{3}{12} = \frac{3}{12}$ 12. $\frac{14}{16} - \frac{2}{16} = \frac{5}{16}$

3. $\frac{5}{4} - \frac{2}{4} = \frac{3}{4}$ 8. $\frac{4}{9} - \frac{1}{9} = \frac{3}{9}$ 13. $\frac{18}{20} - \frac{13}{20} = \frac{11}{20}$

4. $\frac{2}{3} - \frac{1}{3} = \frac{1}{3}$ 9. $\frac{9}{12} - \frac{1}{12} = \frac{4}{12}$ 14. $\frac{13}{15} - \frac{3}{15} = \frac{15}{15}$

5. $\frac{8}{12} - \frac{7}{12} = \frac{1}{12}$ 10. $\frac{7}{8} - \frac{3}{8} = \frac{4}{8}$ 15. $\frac{5}{6} - \frac{3}{6} = \frac{2}{6}$

Who helped write the Declaration of Independence?

Thomas Jefferson

59 — Fractions: Mixed Numbers

A **mixed number** is a number written as a whole number and a fraction, such as $6\frac{3}{8}$.

To change a fraction into a mixed number, divide the denominator (bottom number) into the numerator (top number). Write the remainder over the denominator.

To change a mixed number into a fraction, multiply the denominator by the whole number, add the numerator, and write it on top of the denominator.

Directions: Write each fraction as a mixed number. Write each mixed number as a fraction.

$\frac{21}{6} = 3\frac{3}{6}$ $\frac{24}{5} = 4\frac{4}{5}$ $\frac{10}{3} = 3\frac{1}{3}$ $\frac{21}{4} = 5\frac{1}{4}$

$\frac{11}{6} = 1\frac{5}{6}$ $\frac{11}{4} = 3\frac{1}{4}$ $\frac{12}{5} = 2\frac{2}{5}$ $\frac{10}{4} = 1\frac{2}{4}$

$4\frac{3}{8} = \frac{35}{8}$ $2\frac{1}{3} = \frac{7}{3}$ $4\frac{3}{5} = \frac{23}{5}$ $3\frac{4}{6} = \frac{22}{6}$

$7\frac{1}{4} = \frac{29}{4}$ $2\frac{3}{5} = \frac{13}{5}$ $7\frac{1}{2} = \frac{15}{2}$ $6\frac{5}{7} = \frac{47}{7}$

$\frac{23}{7} = 3\frac{2}{7}$ $8\frac{1}{3} = \frac{25}{3}$ $9\frac{3}{7} = \frac{66}{7}$ $\frac{32}{24} = 1\frac{8}{24}$

60 — Fractions: Adding Mixed Numbers

When adding mixed numbers, add the whole numbers first, then the fractions.

Examples:

$9\frac{1}{3} + 3\frac{1}{3} = 12\frac{2}{3}$ $2\frac{3}{6} + 1\frac{1}{6} = 3\frac{4}{6}$

Directions: Add the number in the center to the number in each surrounding section.

61 — Fractions: Subtracting Mixed Numbers

When subtracting mixed numbers, subtract the fractions first, then the whole numbers.

Directions: Subtract the mixed numbers. The first one is done for you.

$7\frac{7}{8} - 4\frac{4}{8} = 3\frac{3}{8}$ $4\frac{6}{9} - 3\frac{1}{9} = 1\frac{5}{9}$ $4\frac{1}{2} - 3 = 1\frac{1}{2}$ $7\frac{5}{8} - 6\frac{3}{8} = 1\frac{2}{8}$ $6\frac{3}{9} - 1\frac{1}{9} = 5\frac{2}{9}$ $5\frac{3}{4} - 1\frac{1}{4} = 4\frac{2}{4}$

$5\frac{2}{3} - 3\frac{1}{3} = 2\frac{1}{3}$ $4\frac{8}{10} - 3\frac{3}{10} = 1\frac{5}{10}$ $9\frac{8}{9} - 4\frac{3}{9} = 5\frac{5}{9}$ $7\frac{2}{3} - 6\frac{1}{3} = 1\frac{1}{3}$ $7\frac{2}{3} - 5 = 2\frac{2}{3}$ $9\frac{8}{10} - 6\frac{3}{10} = 3\frac{5}{10}$

Sally needs $1\frac{3}{5}$ yards of cloth to make a dress. She has $4\frac{2}{5}$ yards. How much cloth will be left over? $3\frac{2}{5}$ yards

62 — Equivalent Fractions

Equivalent fractions are two different fractions that represent the same number. **Example:** $\frac{1}{2} = \frac{3}{6}$

Directions: Complete these equivalent fractions. Use your fraction pieces from pages 53 and 55.

$\frac{1}{3} = \frac{2}{6}$ $\frac{1}{2} = \frac{4}{8}$ $\frac{3}{4} = \frac{6}{8}$ $\frac{1}{3} = \frac{3}{9}$

Directions: Write the fraction for the shaded area under each figure. Circle the figure that shows a fraction equivalent to figure a.

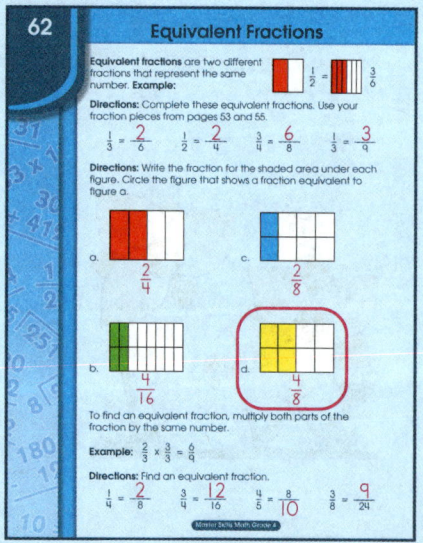

a. $\frac{2}{4}$ c. $\frac{2}{8}$ b. $\frac{4}{16}$ d. $\frac{4}{8}$

To find an equivalent fraction, multiply both parts of the fraction by the same number.

Example: $\frac{2}{3} \times \frac{3}{3} = \frac{6}{9}$

Directions: Find an equivalent fraction.

$\frac{1}{4} = \frac{2}{8}$ $\frac{3}{4} = \frac{12}{16}$ $\frac{4}{5} = \frac{8}{10}$ $\frac{3}{8} = \frac{9}{24}$

63 — Reducing Fractions

Reducing a fraction means finding the greatest common factor and divide.

Example: $\frac{5}{15}$ factors of 5: 1, 5   factors of 15: 1, 3, 5, 15

5 is the greatest common factor. Divide both the numerator and denominator by 5.

$5 \div 5 = 1$ $15 \div 5 = 3$

Directions: Reduce each fraction. Circle the correct answer.

$\frac{2}{4} = \frac{1}{6} \; \textcircled{$\frac{1}{2}$} \; \frac{1}{8}$ $\frac{3}{6} = \textcircled{$\frac{1}{2}$} \; \frac{1}{3} \; \frac{1}{6}$ $\frac{5}{10} = \frac{1}{5} \; \textcircled{$\frac{1}{2}$} \; \frac{5}{6}$

$\frac{4}{12} = \frac{1}{2} \; \textcircled{$\frac{1}{3}$} \; \frac{3}{3}$ $\frac{10}{15} = \frac{1}{3} \; \textcircled{$\frac{2}{3}$} \; \frac{2}{2}$ $\frac{4}{12} = \frac{1}{2} \; \textcircled{$\frac{1}{3}$}$

Directions: Find the way home. Color the boxes with fractions equivalent to $\frac{1}{6}$ or $\frac{1}{3}$.

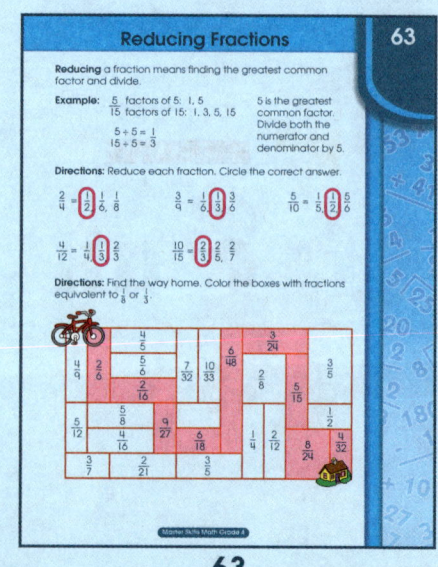

64 — Review

66 — Decimals

68 — Adding and Subtracting Decimals

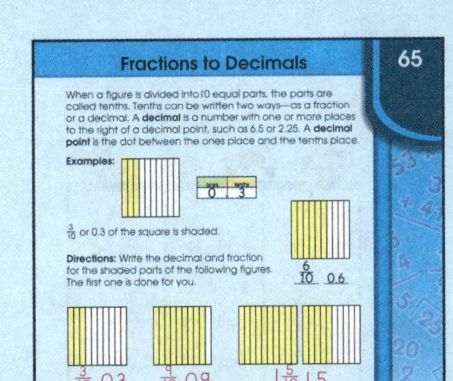

65 — Fractions to Decimals

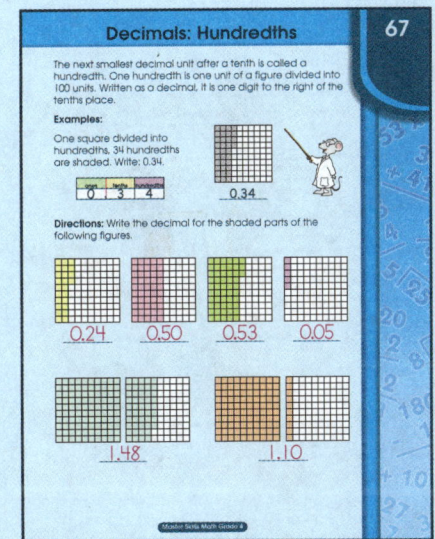

67 — Decimals: Hundredths

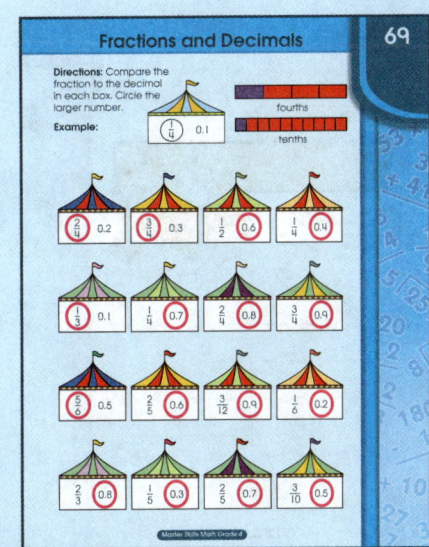

69 — Fractions and Decimals

Answer Key

70 Identifying Operations

Directions: Write the correct operation sign (+, −, ×, ÷) in each circle to correctly complete the problem. The first two are done for you.

5 (×) 6 = 30	0.3 (−) 0.2 = 0.1	128 (−) 56 = 72
4 (×) 8 = 32	$1\frac{3}{8}$ (+) $2\frac{3}{8}$ = $3\frac{6}{8}$	49 (÷) 7 = 7
54 (÷) 6 = 9	$\frac{1}{10}$ (+) $\frac{4}{10}$ = $\frac{5}{10}$	188 (+) 21 = 209
28 (+) 16 = 44	$3\frac{3}{8}$ (−) $2\frac{2}{8}$ = $1\frac{1}{8}$	16 (÷) 4 = 4
63 (÷) 7 = 9	12 (×) 12 = 144	10 (×) 0 = 0
49 (−) 9 = 40	100 (÷) 5 = 20	0.91 (−) 0.81 = 0.1
48 (÷) 12 = 4	98 (−) 43 = 55	0.3 (+) 0.3 = 0.6
39 (−) 19 = 20	0.9 (−) 0.7 = 0.2	0.5 (+) 0.5 = 1.0
72 (÷) 8 = 9	1.68 (−) 0.9 = 0.78	0.97 (+) .50 = 1.47

Master Skills Math Grade 4

70

71 Identifying Operations

Directions: Solve the problems. Circle the letter with the correct answer. Write the letters in order to read the message.

1. 348 − 227 =	121	(M)	425	S
2. 542 × 6 =	5,683	W	3,252	(A)
3. 328 + 593 =	921	(T)	149	N
4. 1,280 ÷ 40 =	92	L	32	(H)
5. 24 × 52 =	2,386	W	1,248	(I)
6. 863 − 438 =	425	(S)	234	U
7. 4,586 + 1,097 =	3,489	Q	5,683	(W)
8. 480 ÷ 4 =	32	H	120	(O)
9. 0.5 + 0.9 =	1.4	(N)	0.14	E
10. 1.6 − 0.9 =	0.7	(D)	0.9	T
11. $3\frac{1}{5} + 2\frac{3}{5}$ =	$5\frac{4}{5}$	(E)	$4\frac{2}{5}$	L
12. $\frac{5}{8} - \frac{1}{4}$ =	$\frac{3}{8}$	Y	$\frac{1}{4}$	(R)
13. 2,193 − 1,864 =	329	(F)	591	Y
14. 26 × 9 =	234	(U)	744	L
15. 42 ÷ 6 =	8	M	7	(L)

M A T H I S
W O N D E R F U L

Master Skills Math Grade 4

71

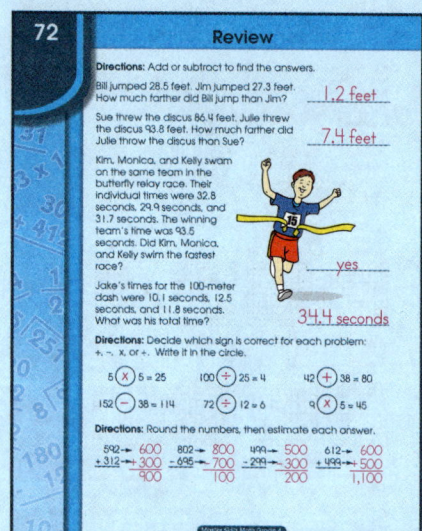

72 Review

Directions: Add or subtract to find the answers.

Bill jumped 28.5 feet. Jim jumped 27.3 feet. How much farther did Bill jump than Jim? 1.2 feet

Sue threw the discus 86.4 feet. Julie threw the discus 93.8 feet. How much farther did Julie throw the discus than Sue? 7.4 feet

Kim, Monica, and Kelly swam on the same team in the butterfly relay race. Their individual times were 32.8 seconds, 29.9 seconds, and 31.7 seconds. The winning team's time was 93.5 seconds. Did Kim, Monica, and Kelly swim the fastest race? yes

Jake's times for the 100-meter dash were 10.1 seconds, 12.5 seconds, and 11.8 seconds. What was his total time? 34.4 seconds

Directions: Decide which sign is correct for each problem: +, −, ×, or ÷. Write it in the circle.

5 (×) 5 = 25 — 100 (÷) 25 = 4 — 42 (+) 38 = 80
152 (−) 38 = 114 — 72 (÷) 12 = 6 — 9 (×) 5 = 45

Directions: Round the numbers, then estimate each answer.

592 → 600, + 312 → + 300 = 900
802 → 800, − 695 → − 700 = 100
499 → 500, − 299 → − 300 = 200
612 → 600, + 499 → + 500 = 1,100

Master Skills Math Grade 4

72

74 Measurement: Inches

Directions: Use a ruler to measure the width of each foot to the nearest inch.

1 in.
3 in.
1 in.
2 in.
1 in.
3 in.
1 in.

Master Skills Math Grade 4

74

75 Measurement: Fractions of an Inch

An inch is divided into smaller units, or fractions of an inch.

Example: This stick of gum is $2\frac{3}{8}$ inches long.

Chewing Gum

Directions: Use a ruler to measure each line to the nearest quarter of an inch. The first one is done for you.

1. $\frac{3}{4}$ inch
2. $1\frac{1}{2}$
3. $2\frac{1}{4}$
4. $4\frac{1}{4}$
5. $3\frac{3}{4}$
6. $1\frac{3}{4}$
7. $3\frac{1}{2}$

Master Skills Math Grade 4

75

76 Measurement: Fractions of an Inch

Directions: Use a ruler to measure to the nearest quarter of an inch.

How far did the grasshopper jump?
$\frac{3}{4} + 1\frac{1}{4} + 1\frac{1}{4} + 2\frac{1}{4} = 5\frac{1}{2}$

What is the total length of the paintbrushes?
$2\frac{1}{2} + 4\frac{1}{4} + 1\frac{1}{4} + 3\frac{1}{4} + 5\frac{1}{4} = 16\frac{1}{2}$

Master Skills Math Grade 4

76

77 — Measurement: Foot, Yard, Mile

Directions: Choose the measure of distance you would use for each object.

1 foot = 12 inches
1 yard = 3 feet
1 mile = 1,760 yards or 5,280 feet

inches
yards
miles
inches
yards
yards
miles

77

78 — Measurement: Perimeter and Area

Perimeter is the distance around a figure. It is found by adding the lengths of the sides. **Area** is the number of square units needed to cover a region. The area is found by adding the number of square units. A unit can be any unit of measure. Most often, inches, feet, or yards are used.

Directions: Find the perimeter and area for each figure. The first one is done for you.

☐ = 1 square unit

Perimeter = 18 units
Area = 17 sq. units

Perimeter = 36 units
Area = 40 sq. units

Perimeter = 24 units
Area = 14 sq. units

Perimeter = 42 units
Area = 46 sq. units

Perimeter = 28 units
Area = 32 sq. units

Perimeter = 42 units
Area = 65 sq. units

78

79 — Measurement: Perimeter

Perimeter is calculated by adding the lengths of the sides of a figure.

Examples:

2 + 2 + 2 + 2 + 6 + 6 = 20
The perimeter of this hexagon is 20 ft.

10 + 10 + 3 + 3 = 26
The perimeter of this parallelogram is 26 yd.

Directions: Find the perimeter of the following figures.

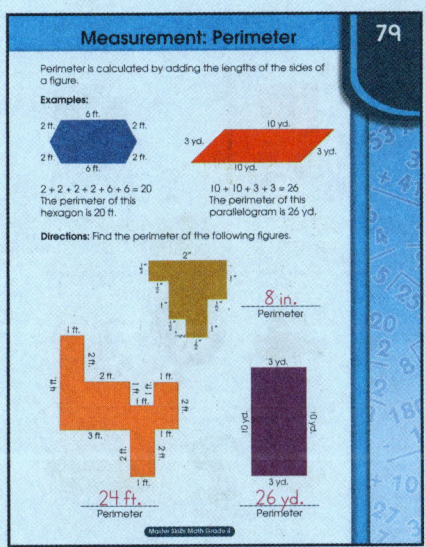

8 in.
Perimeter

24 ft.
Perimeter

26 yd.
Perimeter

79

80 — Measurement: Perimeter and Area

Directions: Calculate the perimeter of each figure.

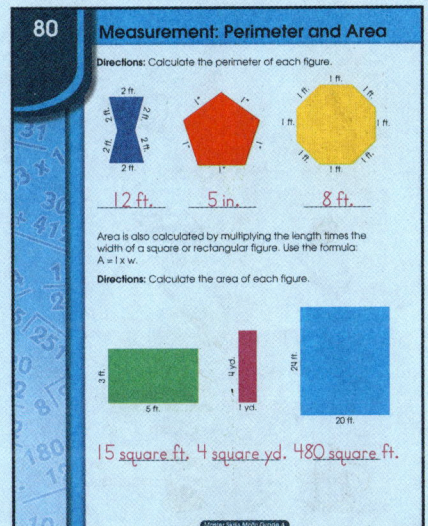

12 ft.   5 in.   8 ft.

Area is also calculated by multiplying the length times the width of a square or rectangular figure. Use the formula: A = l x w.

Directions: Calculate the area of each figure.

15 square ft.   4 square yd.   480 square ft.

80

81 — Measurement: Volume

Volume is the number of cubic units that fit inside a figure.

Directions: Find the volume of each figure. The first one is done for you.

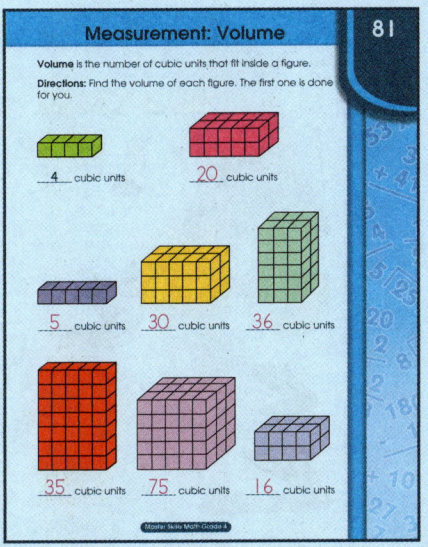

4 cubic units   20 cubic units

5 cubic units   30 cubic units   36 cubic units

35 cubic units   75 cubic units   16 cubic units

81

82 — Measurement: Volume

The volume of a figure can also be calculated by multiplying the length times the width times the height. Use the formula: l x w x h.

Example:
3 x 5 x 2 = 30 cubic feet

Directions: Find the volume of the following figures. Label your answers in feet, inches, or yards. The first one is done for you.

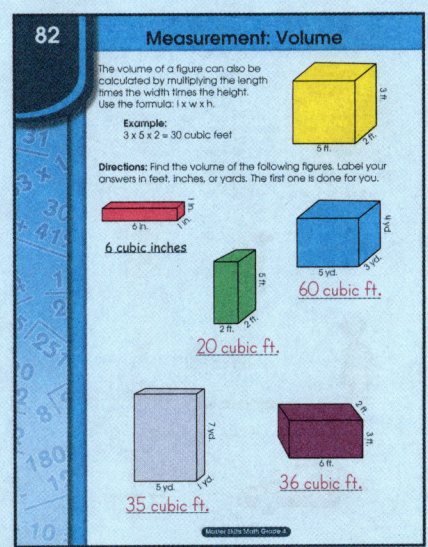

6 cubic inches

60 cubic ft.

20 cubic ft.

35 cubic ft.   36 cubic ft.

82

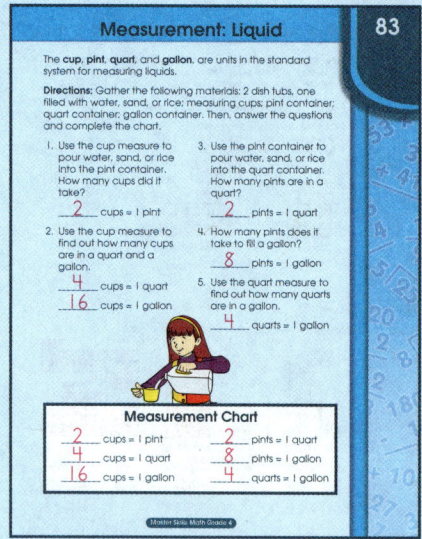

83

Measurement: Liquid

The **cup**, **pint**, **quart**, and **gallon**, are units in the standard system for measuring liquids.

Directions: Gather the following materials: 2 dish tubs, one filled with water, sand, or rice; measuring cups; pint container; quart container; gallon container. Then, answer the questions and complete the chart.

1. Use the cup measure to pour water, sand, or rice into the pint container. How many cups did it take?

   __2__ cups = 1 pint

2. Use the cup measure to find out how many cups are in a quart and a gallon.

   __4__ cups = 1 quart
   __16__ cups = 1 gallon

3. Use the pint container to pour water, sand, or rice into the quart container. How many pints are in a quart?

   __2__ pints = 1 quart

4. How many pints does it take to fill a gallon?

   __8__ pints = 1 gallon

5. Use the quart measure to find out how many quarts are in a gallon.

   __4__ quarts = 1 gallon

Measurement Chart

__2__ cups = 1 pint	__2__ pints = 1 quart
__4__ cups = 1 quart	__8__ pints = 1 gallon
__16__ cups = 1 gallon	__4__ quarts = 1 gallon

83

84

Measurement: Cup, Pint, Quart, Gallon

Directions: Circle the number of objects to the right that equal the objects on the left. The first one is done for you.

84

85

Measurement: Ounce, Pound, Ton

The **ounce**, **pound**, and **ton** are units in the standard system for measuring weight.

ounce   pound   ton

16 ounces = 1 pound   2,000 pounds = 1 ton

Directions: Choose the measure of weight you would use for each object.

Example: __ounces__

__tons/pounds__

__pounds__   __ounces__

__ounces/pounds__   __tons__

__tons__   __pounds__

85

86

Review

Directions: Find the perimeter and area of each figure.

☐ = 1 square unit

Perimeter = __20__ units   Perimeter = __24__ units
Area = __19__ sq. units   Area = __14__ sq. units

Directions: How much does it equal?

= __2__ pints   = __3__ pints

Directions: Write whether you would use ounce, pound, or ton to weigh the following.

__ounces__   __ton__   __pound__

Directions: Write whether you would use an inch, foot, yard, or mile to measure the following.

__inch__   __foot/yard__   __yard__

86

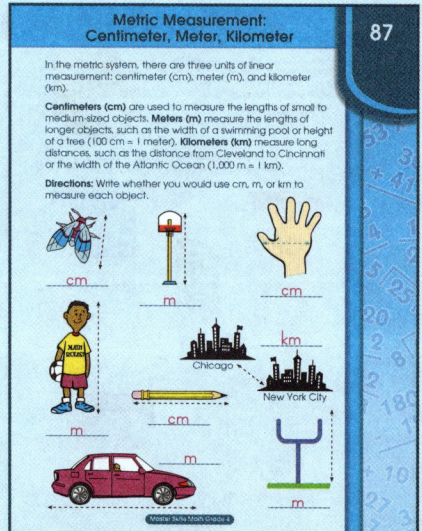

87

Metric Measurement: Centimeter, Meter, Kilometer

In the metric system, there are three units of linear measurement: centimeter (cm), meter (m), and kilometer (km).

Centimeters (cm) are used to measure the lengths of small to medium-sized objects. **Meters (m)** measure the lengths of longer objects, such as the width of a swimming pool or height of a tree (100 cm = 1 meter). **Kilometers (km)** measure long distances, such as the distance from Cleveland to Cincinnati or the width of the Atlantic Ocean (1,000 m = 1 km).

Directions: Write whether you would use cm, m, or km to measure each object.

__cm__   __m__   __cm__

__m__   __km__
Chicago   New York City

__m__   __cm__

__m__   __m__

87

88

Metric Measurement: Centimeter

Directions: Use a centimeter ruler to measure the width of each foot to the nearest centimeter.

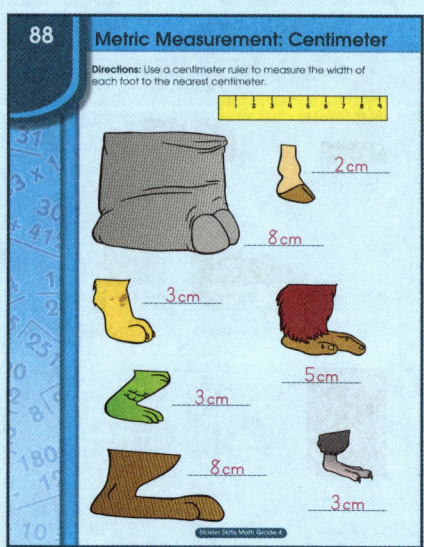

__2 cm__

__8 cm__

__3 cm__

__5 cm__

__3 cm__

__8 cm__

__3 cm__

88

Answer Key

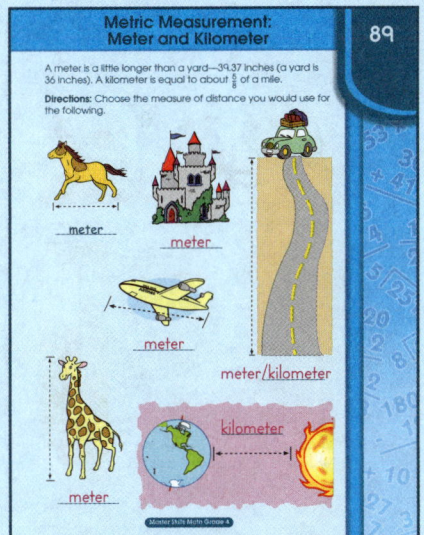

89

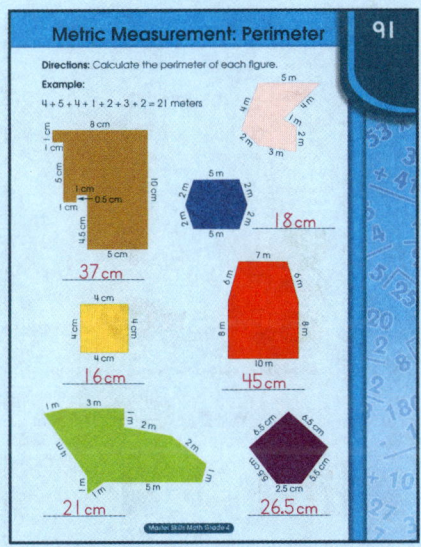

91

93

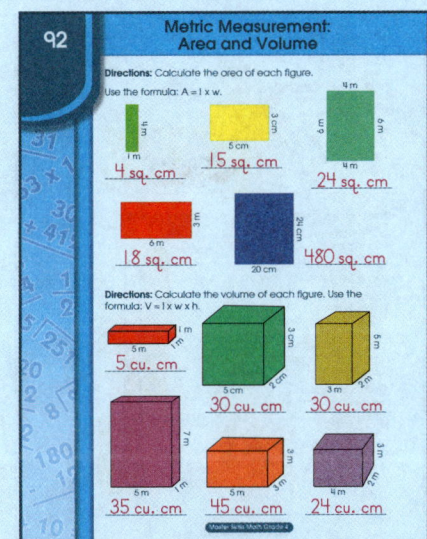

92

94

Answer Key

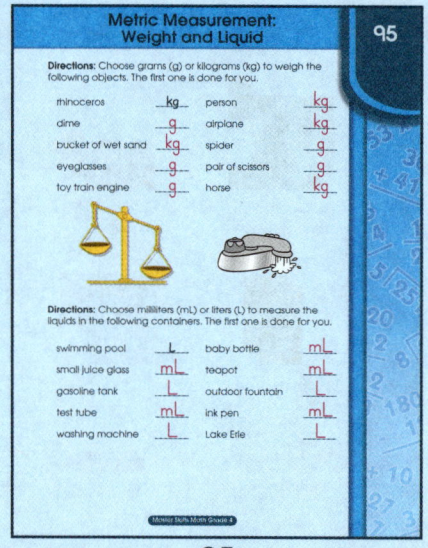

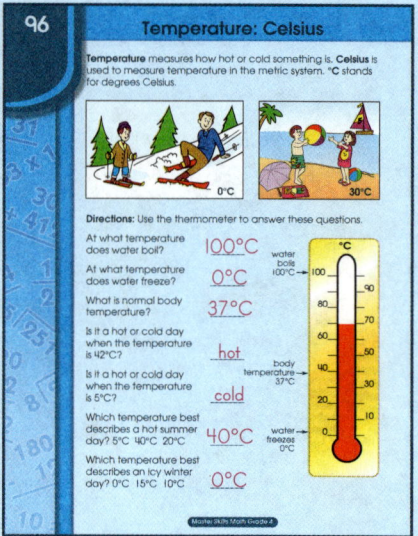

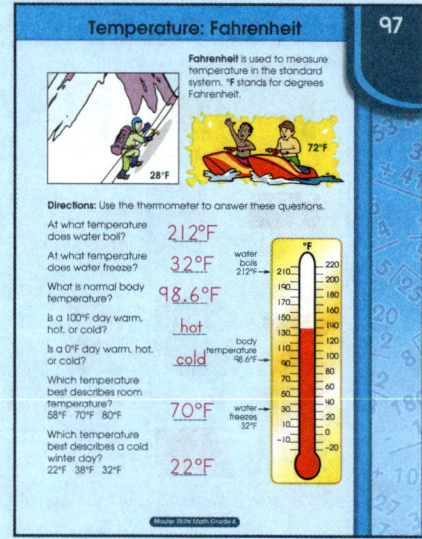

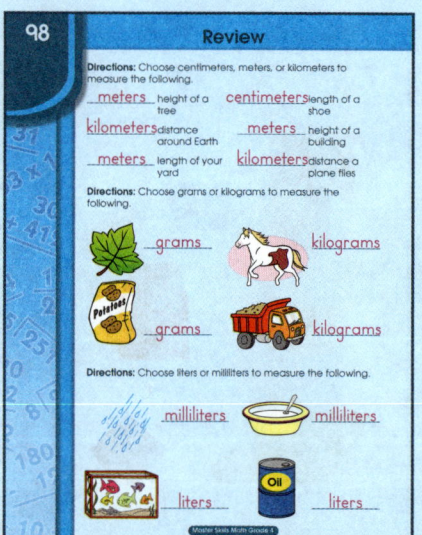

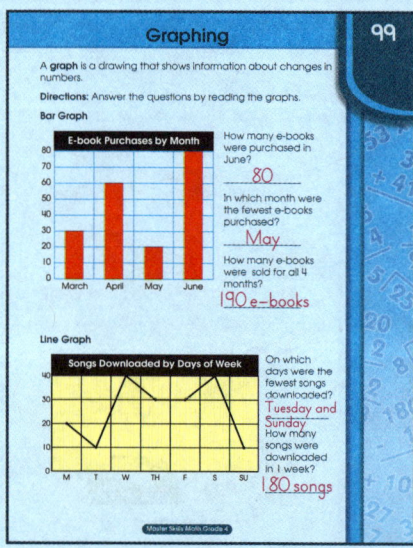

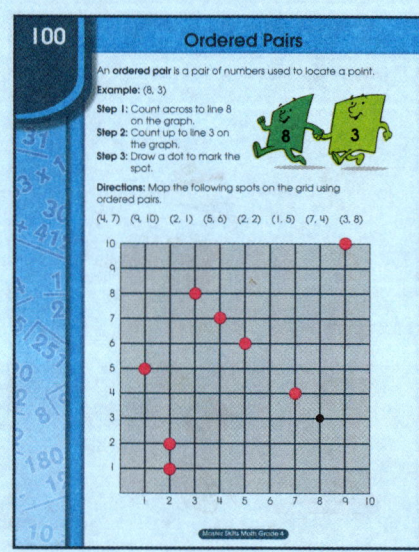

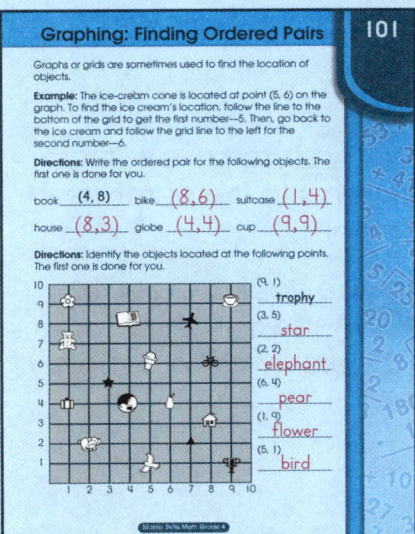

101

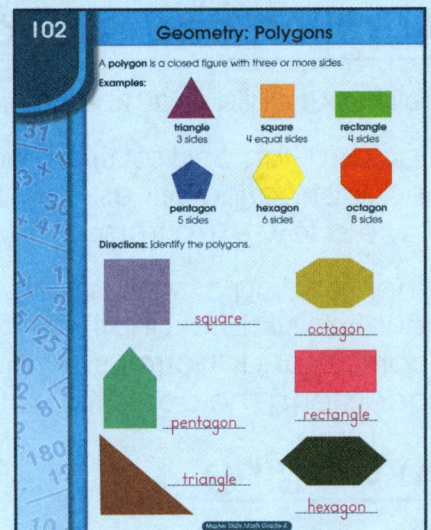

102

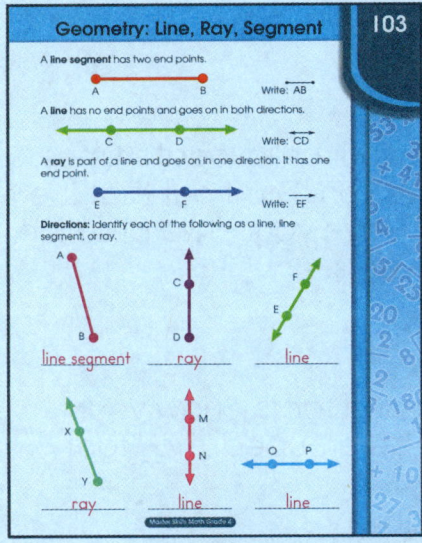

103

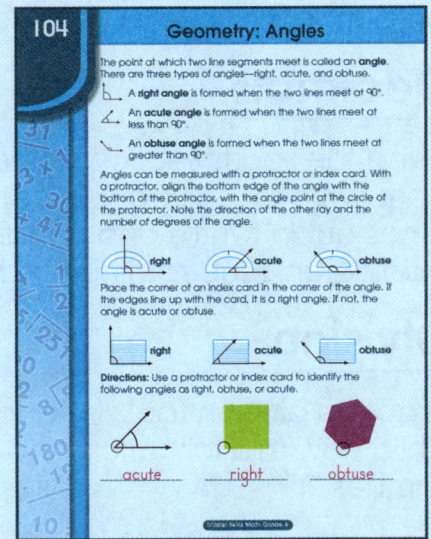

104

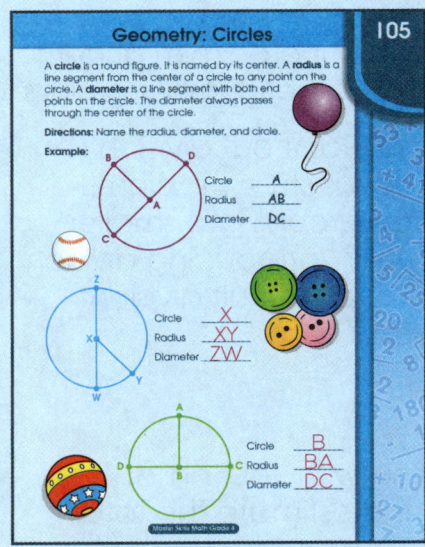

105

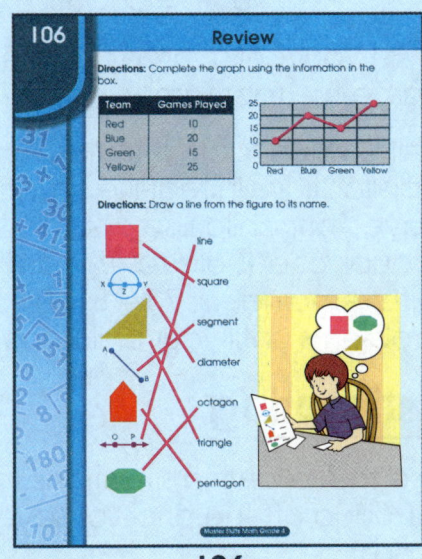

106

Addition and Subtraction

Help your child practice basic facts with flash cards.

Play addition and subtraction games at the grocery store by adding and subtracting prices. Tally the total number of items to be purchased. Place a few extra items in the cart and subtract them.

When adding or subtracting larger numbers, provide your child with counting sticks or another type of manipulative. When your child "carries" and "borrows" with concrete materials, he or she will better understand the operations involved.

Averaging

With your child, brainstorm daily situations in which you use averaging: the cost of groceries for a month, the cost of lunches for a week, the amount of gas used in the car for a month, and so on.

Decimals

Using the sports section of the newspaper, help your child locate times from swim meets, track meets, auto races, and so on. Point out that the times are in tenths and hundredths of seconds. Have your child practice adding and subtracting the times of sporting events.

Division

Practice division facts in tandem with multiplication facts. Show your child how multiplication and division facts can be grouped into "fact families."

Examples: $7 \times 9 = 63$ $9 \times 7 = 63$ $63 \div 7 = 9$ $63 \div 9 = 7$
$6 \times 5 = 30$ $5 \times 6 = 30$ $30 \div 6 = 5$ $30 \div 5 = 6$

Give your child three numbers such as **7, 8**, and **56**, and ask him or her to name the fact family. Have your child practice with other number groups.

Drill division facts with flash cards and oral quizzes. Point out division applications in real-life situations. If mastery of facts is still a problem, have your child use counting sticks to divide large groups into smaller groups of equal size. This activity is also helpful when introducing division with remainders: $73 \div 8 = 9 R1$. Do not go on to more difficult division problems until your child has mastered the basics.

Estimating

Use the following situations to reinforce estimating with your child:
• Round off the price of several grocery items and estimate the total cost.

- Round the total cost at a restaurant and calculate the tip.
- Estimate the number of miles between home and school or other destinations.
- Use a pizza carry-out menu to estimate the costs of pizzas with various toppings.

Fractions

Use foods such as pizza, cake, pie, and brownies to help your child identify halves, fourths, thirds, and so on. Review identification of numerators and denominators. With the foods listed above, practice adding and subtracting like fractions. **Example:** If Sally takes $\frac{1}{6}$ of the pie and Jane takes $\frac{2}{6}$ of the pie, how much of the pie is gone? How much of the pie is left over?

Geometry

Look for shapes in everyday objects. Point out the differences in perpendicular, parallel, and intersecting lines. Show your child that parallel lines are like railroad tracks; perpendicular lines are in room corners; intersecting lines are at some street corners.

Have fun using a compass and protractor to draw circles and designs. Show your child that you set your compass measure for one-half of the size of the desired circle. The compass needs to be set at the radius measure.

Graphing

Show your child that graphing has many practical applications in daily life. Use the business section of the newspaper to practice reading graphs. Have your child identify whether the graph is a line graph, bar graph, or pictograph. Help your child graph: weather for a month; food eaten for a week; favorite books of friends; books read over a specific period of time; favorite colors, music, sports, games; and so on.

Measurement

Help your child see that you use measurement on a daily basis. You measure ingredients for recipes, mileage to and from work and school, and so on. Allow your child to help measure whenever possible. Have him or her find the area and/or volume of his or her room. Send your child on a "measuring safari" equipped with a ruler and a list of objects to measure. Have him or her assist in cooking by measuring ingredients.

Note: Do not make comparisons of standard and metric measures. This will only confuse your child. Standard/metric conversions can be learned at a later time.

Teaching Suggestions

Multiplication

The key to success in multiplication is the mastery of single-digit multiplication facts from 0 to 12. Help your child practice these facts with multiplication flash cards, bingo games, homemade activity sheets, and timed tests. Play multiplication games with number cubes, dice, or spinners. Have your child roll the dice and multiply the two numbers rolled or spun.

Make up multiplication story problems. **Example:** You make 9 cupcakes. On each cupcake you want to place 5 pieces of candy. How many pieces will you need in all?

Place Value

To enhance your child's understanding of place value, have him or her practice counting and grouping craft sticks or toothpicks into bundles of tens, hundreds, and thousands. Have your child manipulate these groupings on a place value chart to make various numbers. After making numbers with manipulatives, your child can write the numbers on the chart.

Rounding

To help build your child's understanding of rounding numbers, make several number lines on adding-machine tape. Number each as follows:

- from 0 to 100, counting by tens (for rounding to the nearest ten).
- from 100 to 1,000, counting by hundreds (for rounding to the nearest hundred).
- from 1,000 to 10,000, counting by thousands (for rounding to the nearest thousand).
- from 10,000 to 100,000, counting by ten thousands (for rounding to the nearest ten thousand).

Skip Counting

To help your child practice skip counting, make a large number line on sheets of construction paper, using one sheet per number. Number the sheets from 0 to 100. As your child practices skip counting, he or she can literally "skip" from one number to the next. The physical movement of skip counting will enhance your child's understanding of this concept.